HAMLET

WITH READER'S GUIDE

AMSCO LITERATURE PROGRAM

WILBERT J. LEVY, *Program Editor*

William Shakespeare

HAMLET

Amsco Literature Program

When ordering this book, you may specify:
R 83 ALP (*Paperback*)
R 83 H (*Hardbound*)

WITH READER'S GUIDE

Henry I. Christ

Amsco School Publications, Inc.
315 HUDSON STREET NEW YORK, N.Y. 10013

ISBN 978-0-87720-801-3 (Paperback)
ISBN 978-0-87720-833-4 (Hardback)

Hamlet with Reader's Guide

Amsco School Publications, Inc.

Printed in the United States of America

CONTENTS

Characters in the Play

Claudius, king of Denmark
Hamlet, son to the late, and nephew to the present king
Polonius, lord chamberlain
Horatio, friend to Hamlet
Laertes, son to Polonius
Voltimand ⎤
Cornelius ⎥
Rosencrantz ⎥
Guildenstern ⎬ courtiers
Osric ⎥
A Gentleman ⎦
A Priest
Marcellus ⎤
Bernardo ⎦ officers
Francisco, a soldier
Reynaldo, servant to Polonius
Players
Two Clowns, grave-diggers
Fortinbras, prince of Norway
A Captain
English Ambassadors

Gertrude, queen of Denmark, and mother to Hamlet
Ophelia, daughter to Polonius

Lords, Ladies, Officers, Soldiers, Sailors, Messengers, and
other Attendants

Ghost of Hamlet's Father

The Tragedy of Hamlet, Prince of Denmark

2 **unfold:**   identify.

6 **carefully upon your hour:**   exactly when you were due.

ACT I

Francisco at his post. Enter to him Bernardo.

Bernardo
Who's there?
Francisco
Nay, answer me: stand, and unfold yourself.
Bernardo
Long live the king!
Francisco
Bernardo?
Bernardo
He.   5
Francisco
You come most carefully upon your hour.
Bernardo
'Tis now struck twelve; get thee to bed, Francisco.
Francisco
For this relief much thanks: 'tis bitter cold,
And I am sick at heart.
Bernardo
Have you had quiet guard?   10
Francisco
                                   Not a mouse stirring.

14 **rivals:** partners.

17 **liegemen to the Dane:** loyal subjects of the King of Denmark.

Bernardo
Well, good night.
If you do meet Horatio and Marcellus,
The rivals of my watch, bid them make haste.
Francisco
I think I hear them. Stand, ho! Who is there?   15

Enter Horatio and Marcellus.

Horatio
Friends to this ground.
Marcellus
                 And liegemen to the Dane.
Francisco
Give you good night.
Marcellus
              O, farewell, honest soldier:
Who hath reliev'd you?   20
Francisco
            Bernardo hath my place.
Give you good night.
                           [*Exit.*
Marcellus
             Holla! Bernardo!
Bernardo
                   Say,
What, is Horatio there?   25
Horatio
             A piece of him.
Bernardo
Welcome, Horatio; welcome, good Marcellus.
Marcellus
What, has this thing appear'd again tonight?
Bernardo
I have seen nothing.

36 **approve our eyes:** verify what we have seen.

39 **assail your ears:** try to convince you.

45 **pole:** polestar.
46 **illume:** brighten.

53 **harrows:** deeply disturbs.

Marcellus

　　Horatio says 'tis but our fantasy,　　　　　　　30
　　And will not let belief take hold of him
　　Touching this dreaded sight, twice seen of us:
　　Therefore I have entreated him along
　　With us to watch the minutes of this night,
　　That if again this apparition come,　　　　　　35
　　He may approve our eyes and speak to it.

Horatio

　　Tush, tush, 'twill not appear.

Bernardo

　　　　　　　　　　　Sit down awhile;
　　And let us once again assail your ears,
　　That are so fortified against our story,　　　　40
　　What we have two nights seen.

Horatio

　　　　　　　　　　Well, sit we down,
　　And let us hear Bernardo speak of this.

Bernardo

　　Last night of all,
　　When yond same star that's westward from the pole　45
　　Had made his course to illume that part of heaven
　　Where now it burns, Marcellus and myself,
　　The bell then beating one—

　　　Enter Ghost.

Marcellus

　　Peace, break thee off; look, where it comes again!

Bernardo

　　In the same figure, like the king that's dead.　　50

Marcellus

　　Thou art a scholar; speak to it, Horatio.

Bernardo

　　Looks it not like the king? mark it, Horatio.

Horatio

　　Most like: it harrows me with fear and wonder.

68 **sensible and true avouch:**   direct evidence.

73 **Norway:**   King of Norway.
74 **parle:**   confrontation.
75 **sledded Polacks:**   variously interpreted as weighted pole-
axe or soldiers (Poles) on sleds

Bernardo
 It would be spoke to.

Marcellus
                        Question it, Horatio.   55

Horatio
 What art thou, that usurp'st this time of night,
 Together with that fair and warlike form
 In which the majesty of buried Denmark
 Did sometimes march? by heaven I charge thee, speak!

Marcellus
 It is offended.   60

Bernardo
                   See, it stalks away!

Horatio
 Stay! speak, speak! I charge thee, speak!
                                            [*Exit Ghost.*

Marcellus
 'Tis gone, and will not answer.

Bernardo
 How now, Horatio! you tremble and look pale:
 Is not this something more than fantasy?   65
 What think you on 't?

Horatio
 Before my God, I might not this believe
 Without the sensible and true avouch
 Of mine own eyes.

Marcellus
                      Is it not like the king?   70

Horatio
 As thou art to thyself:
 Such was the very armor he had on
 When he the ambitious Norway combated;
 So frown'd he once, when, in an angry parle,
 He smote the sledded Polacks on the ice.   75
 'Tis strange.

77 **jump:** exactly.

80 **gross and scope:** general drift.
81 **bodes:** foretells.

82 **Good now:** please.

84 **toils the subject:** wearies the people.

86 **foreign mart:** foreign trade.
87 **impress:** forced service.

96 **emulate:** envious.
97 **Hamlet:** young Hamlet's father, the former King.

103 **moiety competent:** equal part.
104 **gaged:** pledged.
    had: would have.

107 **carriage:** terms.

Marcellus
   Thus twice before, and jump at this dead hour,
   With martial stalk hath he gone by our watch.

Horatio
   In what particular thought to work I know not;
   But, in the gross and scope of my opinion,　　　　　80
   This bodes some strange eruption to our state.

Marcellus
   Good now, sit down, and tell me, he that knows,
   Why this same strict and most observant watch
   So nightly toils the subject of the land,
   And why such daily cast of brazen cannon,　　　　　85
   And foreign mart for implements of war;
   Why such impress of shipwrights, whose sore task
   Does not divide the Sunday from the week;
   What might be toward, that this sweaty haste
   Doth make the night joint-laborer with the day:　　　　　90
   Who is 't that can inform me?

Horatio
                      That can I;
   At least the whisper goes so. Our last king,
   Whose image even but now appear'd to us,
   Was, as you know, by Fortinbras of Norway,　　　　　95
   Thereto prick'd on by a most emulate pride,
   Dar'd to the combat; in which our valiant Hamlet—
   For so this side of our known world esteem'd him—
   Did slay this Fortinbras; who by a seal'd compact,
   Well ratified by law and heraldry,　　　　　100
   Did forfeit, with his life, all those his lands
   Which he stood seiz'd of, to the conqueror:
   Against the which, a moiety competent
   Was gaged by our king; which had return'd
   To the inheritance of Fortinbras,　　　　　105
   Had he been vanquisher; as, by the same covenant
   And carriage of the article design'd,
   His fell to Hamlet. Now, sir, young Fortinbras,

110 **skirts:** outskirts.
111 **shark'd:** snatched (like a shark).
   lawless resolutes: desperate adventurers.
113 **hath a stomach in 't:** calls for courage.

116 **terms compulsatory:** brute force.

120 **romage:** bustle.

124 **question:** subject, origin.

125 **mote:** speck of dirt.
126 **palmy:** flourishing.

131 **moist star:** moon.

134 **precurse:** forerunner.

Of unimproved metal hot and full,
Hath in the skirts of Norway here and there　　110
Shark'd up a list of lawless resolutes,
For food and diet, to some enterprise
That hath a stomach in 't: which is no other—
As it doth well appear unto our state—
But to recover of us, by strong hand　　115
And terms compulsatory, those foresaid lands
So by his father lost: and this, I take it,
Is the main motive of our preparations,
The source of this our watch and the chief head
Of this post-haste and romage in the land.　　120

Bernardo

I think it be no other but e'en so:
Well may it sort, that this portentous figure
Comes armed through our watch, so like the king
That was and is the question of these wars.

Horatio

A mote it is to trouble the mind's eye.　　125
In the most high and palmy state of Rome,
A little ere the mightiest Julius fell,
The graves stood tenantless, and the sheeted dead
Did squeak and gibber in the Roman streets:
As stars with trains of fire and dews of blood,　　130
Disasters in the sun; and the moist star,
Upon whose influence Neptune's empire stands,
Was sick almost to doomsday with eclipse:
And even the like precurse of fierce events,
As harbingers preceding still the fates　　135
And prologue to the omen coming on,
Have heaven and earth together demonstrated
Unto our climatures and countrymen.

Reenter Ghost.

But soft, behold! lo, where it comes again!
I'll cross it, though it blast me. Stay, illusion!　　140

146 **privy to:**   know anything secret about.

149 **uphoarded:**   hoarded.

154 **partisan:**   weapon with a long shaft and blade.

If thou hast any sound, or use of voice,
Speak to me:
If there be any good thing to be done,
That may to thee do ease and grace to me,
Speak to me: 145
If thou art privy to thy country's fate,
Which, happily, foreknowing may avoid,
O, speak!
Or if thou hast uphoarded in thy life
Extorted treasure in the womb of earth,   150
For which, they say, you spirits oft walk in death,
Speak of it: stay, and speak!

                              [*The cock crows.*
                    Stop it, Marcellus.

Marcellus
Shall I strike at it with my partisan?

Horatio
Do, if it will not stand.   155

Bernardo
                    'Tis here!

Horatio
                              'Tis here!

Marcellus
'Tis gone!

                              [*Exit Ghost.*
We do it wrong, being so majestical,
To offer it the show of violence;   160
For it is, as the air, invulnerable,
And our vain blows malicious mockery.

Bernardo
It was about to speak, when the cock crew.

Horatio
And then it started like a guilty thing
Upon a fearful summons. I have heard,   165
The cock, that is the trumpet to the morn,

168 **god of day:**   the sun.

170 **extravagant:**   wandering.
   hies: hurries.
171 **confine:**   place of confinement.
172 **made probation:**   proved.

178 **planets strike:**   planets bring bad fortune (a belief of as-
   trology).

Doth with his lofty and shrill-sounding throat
Awake the god of day, and at his warning,
Whether in sea or fire, in earth or air,
Th' extravagant and erring spirit hies　　　　　170
To his confine: and of the truth herein
This present object made probation.

Marcellus
It faded on the crowing of the cock.
Some say that ever 'gainst that season comes
Wherein our Saviour's birth is celebrated,　　　　　175
The bird of dawning singeth all night long:
And then, they say, no spirit dare stir abroad,
The nights are wholesome, then no planets strike,
No fairy takes nor witch hath power to charm,
So hallow'd and so gracious is the time.　　　　　180

Horatio
So have I heard and do in part believe it.
But look, the morn, in russet mantle clad,
Walks o'er the dew of yon high eastward hill:
Break we our watch up; and by my advice,
Let us impart what we have seen tonight　　　　　185
Unto young Hamlet; for, upon my life,
This spirit, dumb to us, will speak to him:
Do you consent we shall acquaint him with it,
As needful in our loves, fitting our duty?

Marcellus
Let's do 't, I pray; and I this morning know　　　　　190
Where we shall find him most conveniently.

　　　　　　　　　　　　　　　　[*Exeunt.*

2 **green:** fresh.

8 **sometime:** former.
9 **jointress:** sharer in the inheritance.

11 **auspicious, dropping:** cheerful, sad.

13 **dole:** sorrow.

18 **supposal:** estimate.

21 **colleagued with:** allied with, leagued with.

Scene 2. A room of state in the castle

Flourish. Enter the King, Queen, Hamlet, Polonius,
Laertes, Voltimand, Cornelius, Lords, and Attendants

King
　Though yet of Hamlet our dear brother's death
　The memory be green, and that it us befitted
　To bear our hearts in grief and our whole kingdom
　To be contracted in one brow of woe,
　Yet so far hath discretion fought with nature　　　5
　That we with wisest sorrow think on him,
　Together with remembrance of ourselves.
　Therefore our sometime sister, now our queen,
　Th' imperial jointress to this warlike state,
　Have we, as 'twere with a defeated joy—　　　10
　With an auspicious and a dropping eye,
　With mirth in funeral and with dirge in marriage,
　In equal scale weighing delight and dole—
　Taken to wife: nor have we herein barr'd
　Your better wisdoms, which have freely gone　　　15
　With this affair along. For all, our thanks.
　Now follows, that you know, young Fortinbras,
　Holding a weak supposal of our worth,
　Or thinking by our late dear brother's death
　Our state to be disjoint and out of frame,　　　20
　Colleagued with this dream of his advantage,
　He hath not fail'd to pester us with message,
　Importing the surrender of those lands
　Lost by his father, with all bonds of law,
　To our most valiant brother. So much for him.　　　25
　Now for ourself, and for this time of meeting:
　Thus much the business is: we have here writ
　To Norway, uncle of young Fortinbras—
　Who, impotent and bed-rid, scarcely hears
　Of this his nephew's purpose—to suppress　　　30

31 **gait:** action.

38 **delated:** detailed.

44 **Dane:** King of Denmark.
45 **voice:** petition.

His further gait herein; in that the levies,
The lists and full proportions, are all made
Out of his subject: and we here dispatch
You, good Cornelius, and you, Voltimand,
For bearers of this greeting to old Norway,   35
Giving to you no further personal power
To business with the king more than the scope
Of these delated articles allow.
Farewell, and let your haste commend your duty.

Cornelius and Voltimand
In that and all things will we show our duty.   40

King
We doubt it nothing: heartily farewell.
                    [*Exeunt Voltimand and Cornelius.*
And now, Laertes, what's the news with you?
You told us of some suit; what is 't, Laertes?
You cannot speak of reason to the Dane,
And lose your voice: what wouldst thou beg, Laertes,   45
That shall not be my offer, not thy asking?
The head is not more native to the heart,
The hand more instrumental to the mouth,
Than is the throne of Denmark to thy father.
What wouldst thou have, Laertes?   50

Laertes
                    My dread lord,
Your leave and favor to return to France,
From whence though willingly I came to Denmark,
To show my duty in your coronation,
Yet now, I must confess, that duty done,   55
My thoughts and wishes bend again toward France
And bow them to your gracious leave and pardon.

King
Have you your father's leave? What says Polonius?

Polonius
He hath, my lord, wrung from me my slow leave
By laborsome petition, and at last   60

71 **vailed lids:** lowered eyelids.

81 **suspiration:** sighing.

83 **havior:** behavior.

    Upon his will I seal'd my hard consent:
    I do beseech you, give him leave to go.
King
    Take thy fair hour, Laertes; time be thine.
    And thy best graces spend it at thy will!
    But now, my cousin Hamlet, and my son—   65
Hamlet
    [*Aside*] A little more than kin, and less than kind.
King
    How is it that the clouds still hang on you?
Hamlet
    Not so, my lord; I am too much i' the sun.
Queen
    Good Hamlet, cast thy nighted color off,
    And let thine eye look like a friend on Denmark.   70
    Do not for ever with thy vailed lids
    Seek for thy noble father in the dust:
    Thou know'st 'tis common; all that lives must die,
    Passing through nature to eternity.
Hamlet
    Aye, madam, it is common.   75
Queen
                If it be,
    Why seems it so particular with thee?
Hamlet
    Seems, madam! nay, it is; I know not "seems."
    'Tis not alone my inky cloak, good mother,
    Nor customary suits of solemn black,   80
    Nor windy suspiration of forc'd breath,
    No, nor the fruitful river in the eye,
    Nor the dejected havior of the visage,
    Together with all forms, moods, shapes of grief,
    That can denote me truly: these indeed seem,   85
    For they are actions that a man might play:
    But I have that within which passeth show;
    These but the trappings and the suits of woe.

94 **obsequious:**   dutiful.
95 **condolement:**   mourning.

107 **corse:**   corpse.

109 **us:**   me (the royal *we*).

116 **retrograde:**   contrary.
117 **bend you:**   change your mind.

King
    'Tis sweet and commendable in your nature, Hamlet,
    To give these mourning duties to your father: 90
    But, you must know, your father lost a father,
    That father lost, lost his, and the survivor bound
    In filial obligation for some term
    To do obsequious sorrow: but to persevere
    In obstinate condolement is a course   95
    Of impious stubbornness; 'tis unmanly grief:
    It shows a will most incorrect to heaven,
    A heart unfortified, a mind impatient,
    An understanding simple and unschool'd:
    For what we know must be and is as common   100
    As any the most vulgar thing to sense,
    Why should we in our peevish opposition
    Take it to heart? Fie! 'tis a fault to heaven,
    A fault against the dead, a fault to nature,
    To reason most absurd, whose common theme   105
    Is death of fathers, and who still hath cried,
    From the first corse till he that died today,
    "This must be so." We pray you, throw to earth
    This unprevailing woe, and think of us
    As of a father: for let the world take note,   110
    You are the most immediate to our throne,
    And with no less nobility of love
    Than that which dearest father bears his son
    Do I impart toward you. For your intent
    In going back to school in Wittenberg,   115
    It is most retrograde to our desire:
    And we beseech you, bend you to remain
    Here in the cheer and comfort of our eye,
    Our chiefest courtier, cousin and our son.
Queen
    Let not thy mother lose her prayers, Hamlet: 120
    I pray thee, stay with us; go not to Wittenberg.
Hamlet
    I shall in all my best obey you, madam.

127 **jocund health:** happy toast.

129 **rouse:** revel.
bruit: proclaim abroad.

134 **canon:** divine law.

138 **rank:** gross, overripe.

142 **Hyperion:** sun god.
satyr: ugly creature—half goat, half man.
143 **beteem:** permit.

151 **Niobe:** mother who lost all her children; a symbol of
grief.
152 **wants:** lacks.

King

   Why, 'tis a loving and a fair reply:

   Be as ourself in Denmark. Madam, come;

   This gentle and unforc'd accord of Hamlet   125

   Sits smiling to my heart: in grace whereof,

   No jocund health that Denmark drinks today,

   But the great cannon to the clouds shall tell,

   And the king's rouse the heaven shall bruit again,

   Respeaking earthly thunder. Come away.   130

              [*Flourish. Exeunt all but Hamlet.*

Hamlet

   O, that this too too solid flesh would ·melt,

   Thaw and resolve itself into a dew!

   Or that the Everlasting had not fix'd

   His canon 'gainst self-slaughter! O God! God!

   How weary, stale, flat and unprofitable   135

   Seem to me all the uses of this world!

   Fie on 't! ah fie! 'tis an unweeded garden,

   That grows to seed; things rank and gross in nature

   Possess it merely. That it should come to this!

   But two months dead! nay, not so much, not two: 140

   So excellent a king; that was, to this,

   Hyperion to a satyr: so loving to my mother,

   That he might not beteem the winds of heaven

   Visit her face too roughly. Heaven and earth!

   Must I remember? why, she would hang on him,   145

   As if increase of appetite had grown

   By what it fed on: and yet, within a month—

   Let me not think on 't—Frailty, thy name is

       woman!—

   A little month, or ere those shoes were old

   With which she follow'd my poor father's body,   150

   Like Niobe, all tears: why she, even she—

   O God! a beast that wants discourse of reason

   Would have mourn'd longer—married with my uncle,

   My father's brother, but no more like my father

   Than I to Hercules: within a month;   155

157 **galled:** reddened, inflamed.

159 **incestuous:** Church law considered as incest the marriage between a woman and the brother of her dead husband.

166 **change:** exchange.

Ere yet the salt of most unrighteous tears
Had left the flushing in her galled eyes,
She married. O, most wicked speed, to post
With such dexterity to incestuous sheets!
It is not, nor it cannot come to good: 160
But break, my heart, for I must hold my tongue!

Enter Horatio, Marcellus, and Bernardo.

Horatio
Hail to your lordship!
Hamlet
                        I am glad to see you well:
Horatio   or I do forget myself.
Horatio
The same, my lord, and your poor servant ever.   165
Hamlet
Sir, my good friend; I'll change that name with you:
And what make you from Wittenberg, Horatio?
Marcellus?
Marcellus
My good lord?
Hamlet
I am very glad to see you.   170
        [*To Bernardo*]   Good even, sir.
But what, in faith, make you from Wittenberg?
Horatio
A truant disposition, good my lord.
Hamlet
I would not hear your enemy say so,
Nor shall you do my ear that violence,   175
To make it truster of your own report
Against yourself: I know you are no truant.
But what is your affair in Elsinore?
We'll teach you to drink deep ere you depart.
Horatio
My lord, I came to see your father's funeral.   180

183 **hard upon:** soon after.

198 **Season your admiration:** restrain your amazement.
199 **attent:** attentive.

Hamlet
  I pray thee, do not mock me, fellow-student;
  I think it was to see my mother's wedding.
Horatio
  Indeed, my lord, it follow'd hard upon.
Hamlet
  Thrift, thrift, Horatio! the funeral bak'd meats
  Did coldly furnish forth the marriage tables.   185
  Would I had met my dearest foe in heaven
  Or ever I had seen that day, Horatio!
  My father! methinks I see my father.
Horatio
  O where, my lord?
Hamlet
                    In my mind's eye, Horatio.   190
Horatio
  I saw him once; he was a goodly king.
Hamlet
  He was a man, take him for all in all,
  I shall not look upon his like again.
Horatio
  My lord, I think I saw him yesternight.
Hamlet
  Saw? who?   195
Horatio
  My lord, the king your father.
Hamlet
                    The king my father!
Horatio
  Season your admiration for a while
  With an attent ear, till I may deliver,
  Upon the witness of these gentlemen,   200
  This marvel to you.
Hamlet
                    For God's love, let me hear.

207 **at point:** completely.
     cap-a-pe: from head to foot.

211 **truncheon:** staff of authority.

216 **deliver'd:** related.

Horatio
 Two nights together had these gentlemen,
 Marcellus and Bernardo, on their watch,
 In the dead vast and middle of the night,   205
 Been thus encounter'd. A figure like your father,
 Armed at point exactly, cap-a-pe,
 Appears before them, and with solemn march
 Goes slow and stately by them: thrice he walk'd
 By their oppress'd and fear-surprised eyes, 210
 Within his truncheon's length; whilst they, distill'd
 Almost to jelly with the act of fear,
 Stand dumb, and speak not to him. This to me
 In dreadful secrecy impart they did;
 And I with them the third night kept the watch: 215
 Where, as they had deliver'd, both in time,
 Form of the thing, each word made true and good,
 The apparition comes: I knew your father;
 These hands are not more like.

Hamlet
         But where was this? 220

Marcellus
 My lord, upon the platform where we watch'd.

Hamlet
 Did you not speak to it?

Horatio
        My lord, I did.
 But answer made it none: yet once methought
 It lifted up its head and did address 225
 Itself to motion, like as it would speak:
 But even then the morning cock crew loud,
 And at the sound it shrunk in haste away
 And vanish'd from our sight.

Hamlet
        'Tis very strange. 230

235 **hold you:**   do you hold.

242 **beaver:**   visor.

Horatio
  As I do live, my honor'd lord, 'tis true,
  And we did think it writ down in our duty
  To let you know of it.

Hamlet
  Indeed, indeed, sirs, but this troubles me.
  Hold you the watch tonight?   235

Marcellus and Bernardo
            We do, my lord.

Hamlet
  Arm'd, say you?

Marcellus and Bernardo
          Arm'd, my lord.

Hamlet
            From top to toe?

Marcellus and Bernardo
  My lord, from head to foot.   240

Hamlet
Then saw you not his face?

Horatio
  O, yes, my lord; he wore his beaver up.

Hamlet
  What, look'd he frowningly?

Horatio
  A countenance more in sorrow than in anger.

Hamlet
  Pale, or red?   245

Horatio
  Nay, very pale.

Hamlet
        And fix'd his eyes upon you?

Horatio
  Most constantly.

Hamlet
      I would I had been there.

252 **tell:** count.

257 **sable:** rich black fur.

265 **tenable:** kept.

Horatio
It would have much amaz'd you.   250

Hamlet
Very like, very like. Stay'd it long?

Horatio
While one with moderate haste might tell a hundred.

Marcellus and Bernardo
Longer, longer.

Horatio
Not when I saw 't.

Hamlet
His beard was grizzled? no?   255

Horatio
It was, as I have seen it in his life,
A sable silver'd.

Hamlet
I will watch tonight;
Perchance 'twill walk again.

Horatio
I warrant it will.   260

Hamlet
If it assume my noble father's person,
I'll speak to it, though hell itself should gape
And bid me hold my peace. I pray you all,
If you have hitherto conceal'd this sight,
Let it be tenable in your silence still,   265
And whatsoever else shall hap tonight,
Give it an understanding, but no tongue:
I will requite your loves. So fare you well:
Upon the platform, 'twixt eleven and twelve,
I'll visit you,   270

All
Our duty to your honor.

Hamlet
Your loves, as mine to you: farewell.

274 **doubt:** suspect.

3 **convoy is assistant:** messengers are available.

7 **toy in blood:** a passing fancy.
8 **primy nature:** springtime.

10 **suppliance:** amusement.

14 **crescent:** growing.
15 **thews:** muscles, sinews.
temple: body.

[*Exeunt all but Hamlet.*

My father's spirit in arms! all is not well;
I doubt some foul play: would the night were come!
Till then sit still, my soul: foul deeds will rise,   275
Though all the earth o'erwhelm them, to men's eyes.

[*Exit.*

Scene 3. *A room in Polonius's house*

Enter Laertes and Ophelia.

Laertes

My necessaries are embark'd: farewell:
And, sister, as the winds give benefit
And convoy is assistant, do not sleep,
But let me hear from you.

Ophelia

Do you doubt that?   5

Laertes

For Hamlet, and the trifling of his favor,
Hold it a fashion, and a toy in blood,
A violet in the youth of primy nature,
Forward, not permanent, sweet, not lasting,
The perfume and suppliance of a minute;   10
No more.

Ophelia

No more but so?

Laertes

Think it no more:
For nature crescent does not grow alone
In thews and bulk; but, as this temple waxes,   15

18 **cautel:** falseness.
besmirch: soil.

25 **circumscrib'd:** limited.

33 **credent:** credulous.
list: listen to.

39 **chariest:** most careful.

41 **calumnious:** slanderous.
42 **canker galls:** canker-worm injuries.
infants of the spring: young plants.

45 **blastments:** blighting influences.

The inward service of the mind and soul
Grows wide withal. Perhaps he loves you now;
And now no soil nor cautel doth besmirch
The virtue of his will: but you must fear,
His greatness weigh'd, his will is not his own;   20
For he himself is subject to his birth:
He may not, as unvalued persons do,
Carve for himself, for on his choice depends
The safety and health of this whole state,
And therefore must his choice be circumscrib'd   25
Unto the voice and yielding of that body
Whereof he is the head. Then if he says he loves you,
It fits your wisdom so far to believe it
As he in his particular act and place
May give his saying deed; which is no further   30
Than the main voice of Denmark goes withal.
Then weigh what loss your honor may sustain,
If with too credent ear you list his songs,
Or lose your heart, or your chaste treasure open
To his unmaster'd importunity.   35
Fear it, Ophelia, fear it, my dear sister,
And keep you in the rear of your affection,
Out of the shot and danger of desire.
The chariest maid is prodigal enough,
If she unmask her beauty to the moon: 40
Virtue itself 'scapes not calumnious strokes:
The canker galls the infants of the spring
Too oft before their buttons be disclos'd,
And in the morn and liquid dew of youth
Contagious blastments are most imminent.   45
Be wary then; best safety lies in fear:
Youth to itself rebels, though none else near.

Ophelia
I shall th' effect of this good lesson keep,
As watchman to my heart. But, good my brother,
Do not, as some ungracious pastors do,   50

53 **dalliance:** pleasure seeking.
54 **recks not his own rede:** doesn't follow his own advice.

61 **stay'd:** waited.

63 **character:** imprint.
64 **unproportion'd:** unsuitable.

66 **adoption:** worth.

73 **censure:** opinion.

81 **husbandry:** thrift.

Show me the steep and thorny way to heaven,
Whilst, like a puff'd and reckless libertine,
Himself the primrose path of dalliance treads
And recks not his own rede.

Laertes

O, fear me not.   55
I stay too long: but here my father comes.

Enter Polonius.

A double blessing is a double grace;
Occasion smiles upon a second leave.

Polonius
Yet here, Laertes! Aboard, aboard, for shame!
The wind sits in the shoulder of your sail,   60
And you are stay'd for. There; my blessing with thee!
And these few precepts in thy memory
Look thou character. Give thy thoughts no tongue,
Nor any unproportion'd thought his act.
Be thou familiar, but by no means vulgar.   65
Those friends thou hast, and their adoption tried,
Grapple them to thy soul with hoops of steel,
But do not dull thy palm with entertainment
Of each new-hatch'd unfledg'd comrade. Beware
Of entrance to a quarrel; but being in,   70
Bear 't, that th' opposed may beware of thee.
Give every man thy ear, but few thy voice:
Take each man's censure, but reserve thy judgment.
Costly thy habit as thy purse can buy,
But not express'd in fancy; rich, not gaudy: 75
For the apparel oft proclaims the man;
And they in France of the best rank and station
Are of a most select and generous chief in that.
Neither a borrower nor a lender be:
For loan oft loses both itself and friend,   80
And borrowing dulls the edge of husbandry.
This above all: to thine own self be true,

85 **season:** ripen.

95 **Marry:** by the Virgin Mary (a mild oath).
bethought: thought of.

99 **put:** impressed.

104 **tenders:** promises.

And it must follow, as the night the day,
Thou canst not then be false to any man.
Farewell: my blessing season this in thee!   85

Laertes
Most humbly do I take my leave, my lord.

Polonius
The time invites you; go, your servants tend.

Laertes
Farewell, Ophelia, and remember well
What I have said to you.

Ophelia
                    'Tis in my memory lock'd,   90
And you yourself shall keep the key of it.

Laertes
Farewell.

                                        [*Exit.*

Polonius
What is 't, Ophelia, he hath said to you?

Ophelia
So please you, something touching the Lord Hamlet.

Polonius
Marry, well bethought: 95
'Tis told me, he hath very oft of late
Given private time to you, and you yourself
Have of your audience been most free and bounteous:
If it be so—as so 'tis put on me,
And that in way of caution—I must tell you,   100
You do not understand yourself so clearly
As it behoves my daughter and your honor.
What is between you? give me up the truth.

Ophelia
He hath, my lord, of late made many tenders
Of his affection to me.   105

Polonius
Affection! pooh! you speak like a green girl,

107 **unsifted:** untried.

112 **tender:** regard.

114 **tender me:** present me with.

117 **go to:** an exclamation of impatience.

118 **countenance:** support.

120 **springes:** snares.

128 **command to parley:** a request to speak to you.

131 **in few:** in short.

Unsifted in such perilous circumstance.
Do you believe his tenders, as you call them?

Ophelia

I do not know, my lord, what I should think.

Polonius

Marry, I'll teach you: think yourself a baby,   110
That you have ta'en these tenders for true pay,
Which are not sterling. Tender yourself more dearly;
Or—not to crack the wind of the poor phrase,
Running it thus—you'll tender me a fool.

Ophelia

My lord, he hath importun'd me with love   115
In honorable fashion.

Polonius

Aye, fashion you may call it; go to, go to.

Ophelia

And hath given countenance to his speech, my lord,
With almost all the holy vows of heaven.

Polonius

Aye, springes to catch woodcocks. I do know,   120
When the blood burns, how prodigal the soul
Lends the tongue vows: these blazes, daughter,
Giving more light than heat, extinct in both,
Even in their promise, as it is a-making,
You must not take for fire. From this time   125
Be something scanter of your maiden presence;
Set your entreatments at a higher rate
Than a command to parley. For Lord Hamlet,
Believe so much in him, that he is young,
And with a larger tether may he walk   130
Than may be given you: in few, Ophelia,
Do not believe his vows; for they are brokers,
Not of that dye which their investments show,
But mere implorators of unholy suits,
Breathing like sanctified and pious bawds,   135
The better to beguile. This is for all:

1 **shrewdly:** piercingly.

2 **eager:** sharp.

9 **takes his rouse:** carouses.
10 **wassail:** drinking bout.
   up-spring: wild dance.
11 **Rhenish:** Rhine wine.

I would not, in plain terms, from this time forth,
Have you so slander any moment leisure,
As to give words or talk with the Lord Hamlet.
Look to 't, I charge you: come your ways.   140
Ophelia
I shall obey, my lord.

[*Exeunt.*

Scene 4. The platform

Enter Hamlet, Horatio, and Marcellus.

Hamlet
The air bites shrewdly; it is very cold.
Horatio
It is a nipping and an eager air.
Hamlet
What hour now?
Horatio
                    I think it lacks of twelve.
Marcellus
No, it is struck.   5
Horatio
Indeed? I heard it not: it then draws near the season
Wherein the spirit held his wont to walk.
                    [A *flourish of trumpets, and*
                    ordnance shot off within.
What doth this mean, my lord?
Hamlet
The king doth wake tonight and takes his rouse,
Keeps wassail, and the swaggering up-spring reels; 10
And as he drains his draughts of Rhenish down,

13 **pledge:** toast.

18 **breach:** neglect.

20 **tax'd:** criticized.
21 **clepe:** call.
22 **addition:** title, reputation.

24 **attribute:** reputation.

26 **mole:** defect.

30 **pales:** defenses, fortifications.
31 **o'erleavens:** changes.
32 **plausive:** pleasing.

34 **nature's livery:** uniform given by nature.
    fortune's star: predestined.

The kettle-drum and trumpet thus bray out
The triumph of his pledge.

Horatio

                      Is it a custom?

Hamlet

Aye, marry, is 't: 15
But to my mind, though I am native here
And to the manner born, it is a custom
More honor'd in the breach than the observance.
This heavy-headed revel east and west
Makes us traduc'd and tax'd of other nations: 20
They clepe us drunkards, and with swinish phrase
Soil our addition; and indeed it takes
From our achievements, though perform'd at height,
The pith and marrow of our attribute.
So, oft it chances in particular men,   25
That for some vicious mole of nature in them,
As, in their birth—wherein they are not guilty,
Since nature cannot choose his origin—
By the o'ergrowth of some complexion,
Oft breaking down the pales and forts of reason,   30
Or by some habit that too much o'erleavens
The form of plausive manners, that these men—
Carrying, I say, the stamp of one defect,
Being nature's livery, or fortune's star—
Their virtues else—be they as pure as grace,   35
As infinite as man may undergo—
Shall in the general censure take corruption
From that particular fault: the dram of evil
Doth all the noble substance of a doubt
To his own scandal.   40

     Enter Ghost.

Horatio

                Look, my lord, it comes!

43 **spirit of health:**   blessed spirit.

46 **questionable:**   inviting question.

50 **canoniz'd:**   sanctified.
51 **cerements:**   grave clothes.

58 **disposition:**   nature.

62 **impartment:**   communication.

65 **removed:**   secluded.

Hamlet

　Angels and ministers of grace defend us!
　Be thou a spirit of health or goblin damn'd,
　Bring with thee airs from heaven or blasts from hell,
　Be thy intents wicked or charitable,　　　　　　　45
　Thou com'st in such a questionable shape
　That I will speak to thee: I'll call thee Hamlet,
　King, father, royal Dane: O, answer me!
　Let me not burst in ignorance; but tell
　Why thy canoniz'd bones, hearsed in death,　　　50
　Have burst their cerements; why the sepulcher,
　Wherein we saw thee quietly inurn'd,
　Hath op'd his ponderous and marble jaws,
　To cast thee up again. What may this mean,
　That thou, dead corse, again, in complete steel,　55
　Revisit'st thus the glimpses of the moon,
　Making night hideous; and we fools of nature
　So horridly to shake our disposition
　With thoughts beyond the reaches of our souls?
　Say, why is this? wherefore? what should we do?　60
　　　　　　　　　　[*Ghost beckons Hamlet.*

Horatio

　It beckons you to go away with it,
　As if it some impartment did desire
　To you alone.

Marcellus

　　　　　　Look, with what courteous action
　It waves you to a more removed ground:　　　　65
　But do not go with it.

Horatio

　　　　　　No, by no means.

Hamlet

　It will not speak; then I will follow it.

Horatio

　Do not, my lord.

71 **pin's fee:** worth of a pin.

77 **beetles:** projects.

81 **toys:** fancies.

92 **Nemean lion:** beast slain as one of the Twelve Labors of Hercules.
94 **lets:** hinders.

Hamlet

　　　　　　　　　Why, what should be the fear?　　70
I do not set my life at a pin's fee;
And for my soul, what can it do to that,
Being a thing immortal as itself?
It waves me forth again: I'll follow it.

Horatio

What if it tempt you toward the flood, my lord,　　75
Or to the dreadful summit of the cliff
That beetles o'er his base into the sea,
And there assume some other horrible form,
Which might deprive your sovereignty of reason
And draw you into madness? think of it:　　　80
The very place puts toys of desperation,
Without more motive, into every brain
That looks so many fathoms to the sea
And hears it roar beneath.

Hamlet

　　　　　　　　　It waves me still.　　85
Go on; I'll follow thee.

Marcellus

You shall not go, my lord.

Hamlet

　　　　　　　　　Hold off your hands.

Horatio

Be rul'd; you shall not go.

Hamlet

　　　　　　　　　My fate cries out,　　90
And makes each petty artery in this body
As hardy as the Nemean lion's nerve.
Still am I call'd, unhand me, gentlemen;
By heaven, I'll make a ghost of him that lets me:
I say, away! Go on; I'll follow thee.　　　95
　　　　　　　　[*Exeunt Ghost and Hamlet.*

Horatio

He waxes desperate with imagination.

98 **issue:** result.

Marcellus
  Let's follow; 'tis not fit thus to obey him.
Horatio
  Have after. To what issue will this come?
Marcellus
  Something is rotten in the state of Denmark.
Horatio
  Heaven will direct it.	100
Marcellus
                Nay, let's follow him.
                              [Exeunt.

Scene 5. Another part of the platform

Enter Ghost and Hamlet.

Hamlet
  Whither wilt thou lead me? speak; I'll go no further.
Ghost
  Mark me.
Hamlet
                I will.
Ghost
                My hour is almost come,
  When I to sulphurous and tormenting flames	5
  Must render up myself.
Hamlet
                Alas, poor ghost!
Ghost
  Pity me not, but lend thy serious hearing
  To what I shall unfold.
Hamlet
                Speak; I am bound to hear.	10

21 **spheres:** orbits.

24 **porpentine:** porcupine.
25 **blazon:** revelation.

31 **in the best:** at best.

Ghost
　So art thou to revenge, when thou shalt hear.

Hamlet
　What?

Ghost
　I am thy father's spirit;
　Doom'd for a certain term to walk the night,
　And for the day confin'd to fast in fires,　　　　15
　Till the foul crimes done in my days of nature
　Are burnt and purg'd away. But that I am forbid
　To tell the secrets of my prison-house,
　I could a tale unfold whose lightest word
　Would harrow up thy soul, freeze thy young blood,　　20
　Make thy two eyes, like stars, start from their spheres,
　Thy knotted and combined locks to part
　And each particular hair to stand an end,
　Like quills upon the fretful porpentine:
　But this eternal blazon must not be　　　　25
　To ears of flesh and blood. List, list, O, list!
　If thou didst ever thy dear father love—

Hamlet
　O God!

Ghost
　Revenge his foul and most unnatural murder.

Hamlet
　Murder!　　　　30

Ghost
　Murder most foul, as in the best it is,
　But this most foul, strange, and unnatural.

Hamlet
　Haste me to know 't, that I, with wings as swift
　As meditation or the thoughts of love,
　May sweep to my revenge.　　　　35

Ghost
　　　　　　　　　　I find thee apt;

38 **Lethe wharf:** In Greek mythology, Lethe was the river of forgetfulness.

42 **process:** report.

47 **adulterate:** adulterous.

67 **secure:** safe, unsuspecting.
68 **hebenon:** a poison.

And duller shouldst thou be than the fat weed
That roots itself in ease on Lethe wharf,
Wouldst thou not stir in this. Now, Hamlet, hear:
'Tis given out that, sleeping in my orchard,   40
A serpent stung me; so the whole ear of Denmark
Is by a forged process of my death
Rankly abus'd: but know, thou noble youth,
The serpent that did sting thy father's life
Now wears his crown.   45

Hamlet
                    O my prophetic soul!
My uncle!

Ghost
Aye, that incestuous, that adulterate beast,
With witchcraft of his wit, with traitorous gifts—
O wicked wit and gifts, that have the power   50
So to seduce!—won to his shameful lust
The will of my most seeming-virtuous queen:
O Hamlet, what a falling-off was there!
From me, whose love was of that dignity
That it went hand in hand even with the vow   55
I made to her in marriage; and to decline
Upon a wretch, whose natural gifts were poor
To those of mine!
But virtue, as it never will be mov'd,
Though lewdness court it in a shape of heaven,   60
So lust, though to a radiant angel link'd,
Will sate itself in a celestial bed
And prey on garbage.
But, soft! methinks I scent the morning air;
Brief let me be. Sleeping within my orchard,   65
My custom always of the afternoon,
Upon my secure hour thy uncle stole,
With juice of cursed hebenon in a vial,
And in the porches of my ears did pour
The leperous distilment; whose effect   70

74 **posset:** curdle.
75 **eager:** sharp, sour.

77 **tetter:** diseased thickening of the skin.
 bark'd about: grew like bark around.
78 **lazar-like:** like a leper.

83 **unhousel'd:** without having received the Sacrament.
 disappointed: unprepared.
 unaneled: not having received the last rites.

95 **matin:** morning.

103 **distracted globe:** disturbed brain.
104 **table:** tablet.

Holds such an enmity with blood of man
That swift as quicksilver it courses through
The natural gates and alleys of the body;
And with a sudden vigor it doth posset
And curd, like eager droppings into milk,   75
The thin and wholesome blood: so did it mine;
And a most instant tetter bark'd about,
Most lazar-like, with vile and loathsome crust,
All my smooth body.
Thus was I, sleeping, by a brother's hand   80
Of life, of crown, of queen, at once dispatch'd:
Cut off even in the blossoms of my sin,
Unhousel'd, disappointed, unaneled;
No reckoning made, but sent to my account
With all my imperfections on my head: 85
O, horrible! O, horrible! most horrible!
If thou hast nature in thee, bear it not;
Let not the royal bed of Denmark be
A couch for luxury, and damned incest.
But, howsoever thou pursuest this act,   90
Taint not thy mind, nor let thy soul contrive
Against thy mother aught: leave her to heaven,
And to those thorns that in her bosom lodge,
To prick and sting her. Fare thee well at once!
The glow-worm shows the matin to be near,   95
And 'gins to pale his uneffectual fire:
Adieu, adieu, adieu! remember me.

                                            [*Exit.*

Hamlet
O all you host of heaven! O earth! what else?
And shall I couple hell? O, fie! Hold, hold, my heart;
And you, my sinews, grow not instant old,   100
But bear me stiffly up. Remember thee!
Aye, thou poor ghost, while memory holds a seat
In this distracted globe. Remember thee!
Yea, from the table of my memory
I'll wipe away all trivial fond records,   105

106 **saws:** sayings.

113 **meet:** appropriate.

121 **secure:** protect.

All saws of books, all forms, all pressures past,
That youth and observation copied there;
And thy commandment all alone shall live
Within the book and volume of my brain,
Unmix'd with baser matter: yes, by heaven!   110
O most pernicious woman!
O villain, villain, smiling, damned villain!
My tables—meet it is I set it down,
That one may smile, and smile, and be a villain;
At least I'm sure it may be so in Denmark.   115
                                        [*Writing.*
So, uncle, there you are. Now to my word;
It is "Adieu, adieu! remember me."
I have sworn 't.
Horatio and Marcellus
[*Within*]   My lord, my lord!

       Enter Horatio and Marcellus.

Marcellus
                         Lord Hamlet!   120
Horatio
                              Heaven secure him!
Hamlet
   So be it!
Marcellus
   Illo, ho, ho, my lord!
Hamlet
   Hillo, ho, ho, boy! come, bird, come.
Marcellus
   How is 't, my noble lord?   125
Horatio
                    What news, my lord?
Hamlet
   O, wonderful!
Horatio
   Good my lord, tell it.

136 **arrant:** thoroughgoing.

Hamlet
> No; you will reveal it.

Horatio
> Not I, my lord, by heaven.   130

Marcellus
> Nor I, my lord.

Hamlet
> How say you, then; would heart of man once think it?
> But you'll be secret?

Horatio and Marcellus
> Aye, by heaven, my lord.

Hamlet
> There's ne'er a villain dwelling in all Denmark   135
> But he's an arrant knave.

Horatio
> There needs no ghost, my lord, come from the grave
> To tell us this.

Hamlet
> Why, right; you are i' the right;
> And so, without more circumstance at all,   140
> I hold it fit that we shake hands and part:
> You, as your business and desire shall point you;
> For every man hath business and desire,
> Such as it is; and for my own poor part,
> Look you, I'll go pray.   145

Horatio
> These are but wild and whirling words, my lord.

Hamlet
> I'm sorry they offend you, heartily;
> Yes, faith, heartily.

Horatio
> There's no offense, my lord.

Hamlet
> Yes, by Saint Patrick, but there is, Horatio,   150
> And much offense too. Touching this vision here,

168 **truepenny:**   honest fellow.
169 **cellarage:**   cellar.

It is an honest ghost, that let me tell you:
For your desire to know what is between us,
O'ermaster 't as you may. And now, good friends,
As you are friends, scholars and soldiers,   155
Give me one poor request.

Horatio
What is 't, my lord? we will.

Hamlet
Never make known what you have seen tonight.

Horatio and Marcellus
My lord, we will not.

Hamlet
                              Nay, but swear 't.   160

Horatio
                                        In faith,
My lord, not I.

Marcellus
                    Nor I, my lord, in faith.

Hamlet
Upon my sword.

Marcellus
                    We have sworn, my lord, already.   165

Hamlet
Indeed, upon my sword, indeed.

Ghost
[*Beneath*]   Swear.

Hamlet
Ah, ha, boy! say'st thou so? art thou there, truepenny?
Come on: you hear this fellow in the cellarage:
Consent to swear.   170

Horatio
                    Propose the oath, my lord.

Hamlet
Never to speak of this that you have seen,
Swear by my sword.

175 **Hic et ubique:** here and everywhere.

182 **pioner:** pioneer, miner.

191 **antic disposition:** fantastic appearance.

196 **list:** wanted.

Ghost

  [*Beneath*]   Swear.

Hamlet

  Hic et ubique? then we'll shift our ground.   175
  Come hither, gentlemen,
  And lay your hands again upon my sword:
  Never to speak of this that you have heard,
  Swear by my sword.

Ghost

  [*Beneath*]   Swear.   180

Hamlet

  Well said, old mole! canst work i' th' earth so fast?
  A worthy pioner! Once more remove, good friends.

Horatio

  O day and night, but this is wondrous strange!

Hamlet

  And therefore as a stranger give it welcome.
  There are more things in heaven and earth, Horatio,   185
  Than are dreamt of in your philosophy.
  But come;
  Here, as before, never, so help you mercy,
  How strange or odd soe'er I bear myself,
  As I perchance hereafter shall think meet   190
  To put an antic disposition on,
  That you, at such times seeing me, never shall,
  With arms encumber'd thus, or this head-shake,
  Or by pronouncing of some doubtful phrase,
  As "Well, well, we know," or "We could, an if we
      would,"   195
  Or "If we list to speak," or "There be, an if they
      might,"
  Or such ambiguous giving out, to note
  That you know aught of me: this not to do,
  So grace and mercy at your most need help you,
  Swear.   200

206 **friending:** friendliness.

Ghost
  [*Beneath*]   Swear.
Hamlet
  Rest, rest, perturbed spirit!

                                      [*They swear.*
              So, gentlemen,
  With all my love I do commend me to you:
  And what so poor a man as Hamlet is   205
  May do, to express his love and friending to you,
  God willing, shall not lack. Let us go in together;
  And still your fingers on your lips, I pray.
  The time is out of joint: O cursed spite,
  That ever I was born to set it right!   210
  Nay, come, let's go together.
                                      [*Exeunt.*

ACT II

Scene 1. A room in Polonius's house

Enter Polonius and Reynaldo.

Polonius
  Give him this money and these notes, Reynaldo.
Reynaldo
  I will, my lord.
Polonius
  You shall do marvelous wisely, good Reynaldo,
  Before you visit him, to make inquire
  Of his behavior.   5
Reynaldo
            My lord, I did intend it.

8 **inquire me:** find out for me.
  Danskers: Danes.

11 **encompassment:** circumvention, roundabout way of finding out.

21 **forgeries:** false reports.

30 **season it in the charge:** tone it down in the telling.

33 **quaintly:** skillfully.

Polonius
  Marry, well said, very well said. Look you, sir,
  Inquire me first what Danskers are in Paris,
  And how, and who, what means, and where they keep,
  What company, at what expense, and finding   10
  By this encompassment and drift of question
  That they do know my son, come you more nearer
  Than your particular demands will touch it:
  Take you, as 'twere, some distant knowledge of him,
  As thus, "I know his father and his friends,   15
  And in part him": do you mark this, Reynaldo?

Reynaldo
  Aye, very well, my lord.

Polonius
  "And in part him; but" you may say, "not well:
  But if 't be he I mean, he's very wild,
  Addicted so and so"; and there put on him   20
  What forgeries you please; marry, none so rank
  As may dishonor him; take heed of that;
  But, sir, such wanton, wild and usual slips
  As are companions noted and most known
  To youth and liberty.   25

Reynaldo
                As gaming, my lord.

Polonius
  Aye, or drinking, fencing, swearing, quarreling,
  Drabbing: you may go so far.

Reynaldo
  My lord, that would dishonor him.

Polonius
  Faith, no; as you may season it in the charge.   30
  You must not put another scandal on him,
  That he is open to incontinency;
  That's not my meaning: but breathe his faults so
       quaintly
  That they may seem the taints of liberty,

36 **unreclaimed:** untamed, wild.
37 **general assault:** a common weakness.

42 **drift:** purpose.
43 **fetch of warrant:** justifiable strategem.

47 **party in converse:** person you are speaking to.
48 **prenominate:** aforesaid, previously mentioned.

50 **closes with:** agrees with.

52 **addition:** title.

The flash and outbreak of a fiery mind,   35
A savageness in unreclaimed blood,
Of general assault.

Reynaldo

          But, my good lord—

Polonius

Wherefore should you do this?

Reynaldo

            Aye, my lord,   40
I would know that.

Polonius

          Marry, sir, here's my drift,
And I believe it is a fetch of warrant:
You laying these slight sullies on my son,
As 'twere a thing a little soil'd i' the working,   45
Mark you,
Your party in converse, him you would sound,
Having ever seen in the prenominate crimes
The youth you breathe of guilty, be assur'd
He closes with you in this consequence;   50
"Good sir," or so, or "friend," or "gentleman,"
According to the phrase or the addition
Of man and country.

Reynaldo

          Very good, my lord.

Polonius

And then, sir, does he this—he does—what was I   55
about to say? By the mass, I was about to say something: where did I leave?

Reynaldo

At "closes in the consequence," at "friend or so," and
"gentleman."

Polonius

At "closes in the consequence," aye, marry;   60
He closes with you thus: "I know the gentleman;

64 **o'ertook in 's rouse:**   overcome by drink.

67 **videlicet:**   namely, that is to say.

71 **windlasses:**   winding, indirect ways.
   assays of bias: indirect aims.

74 **have me:**   understand me.

80 **ply his music:**   go his own way.

I saw him yesterday, or t'other day,
Or then, or then, with such, or such, and, as you say,
There was a' gaming, there o'ertook in 's rouse,
There falling out at tennis:" or perchance,　　65
"I saw him enter such a house of sale,"
Videlicet, a brothel, or so forth.
See you now;
Your bait of falsehood takes this carp of truth:
And thus do we of wisdom and of reach,　　70
With windlasses and with assays of bias,
By indirections find directions out:
So, by my former lecture and advice,
Shall you my son. You have me, have you not?

Reynaldo
My lord, I have.　　75

Polonius
　　　　　　God be wi' ye; fare ye well.

Reynaldo
Good, my lord!

Polonius
Observe his inclination in yourself.

Reynaldo
I shall, my lord.

Polonius
And let him ply his music.　　80

Reynaldo
　　　　　　Well, my lord.

Polonius
Farewell!

　　　　　　　　　　[*Exit Reynaldo.*

　Enter Ophelia.

　　　　How now, Ophelia! what's the matter?

Ophelia
O, my lord, my lord, I have been so affrighted!

86 **closet:** room.

89 **down-gyved:** pulled down, hanging.

113 **ecstasy:** madness.

Polonius
    With what, i' the name of God?   85
Ophelia
    My lord, as I was sewing in my closet,
    Lord Hamlet, with his doublet all unbrac'd,
    No hat upon his head, his stockings foul'd,
    Ungarter'd and down-gyved to his ankle;
    Pale as his shirt, his knees knocking each other,   90
    And with a look so piteous in purport
    As if he had been loosed out of hell
    To speak of horrors, he comes before me.
Polonius
    Mad for thy love?
Ophelia
                        My lord, I do not know,   95
    But truly I do fear it.
Polonius
                        What said he?
Ophelia
    He took me by the wrist and held me hard;
    Then goes he to the length of all his arm,
    And with his other hand thus o'er his brow,   100
    He falls to such perusal of my face
    As he would draw it. Long stay'd he so;
    At last, a little shaking of mine arm,
    And thrice his head thus waving up and down,
    He rais'd a sigh so piteous and profound   105
    As it did seem to shatter all his bulk
    And end his being: that done, he lets me go:
    And with his head over his shoulder turn'd,
    He seem'd to find his way without his eyes;
    For out o' doors he went without their helps,   110
    And to the last bended their light on me.
Polonius
    Come, go with me: I will go seek the king.
    This is the very ecstasy of love;

114 **fordoes:** destroys.

124 **quoted:** observed, noted.
125 **beshrew my jealousy:** curse my suspicion.

2 **moreover that:** besides the fact.

Whose violent property fordoes itself
And leads the will to desperate undertakings   115
As oft as any passion under heaven
That does afflict our natures. I am sorry.
What, have you given him any hard words of late?

Ophelia

No, my good lord, but, as you did command,
I did repel his letters and denied   120
His access to me.

Polonius

                    That hath made him mad.
I am sorry that with better heed and judgment
I had not quoted him: I fear'd he did but trifle
And meant to wreck thee; but beshrew my jealousy!   125
By heaven, it is as proper to our age
To cast beyond ourselves in our opinions
As it is common for the younger sort
To lack discretion. Come, go we to the king:
This must be known; which, being kept close, might move   130
More grief to hide than hate to utter love.
Come.

                              [*Exeunt.*

Scene 2. A room in the castle

*Flourish. Enter King, Queen, Rosencrantz,
Guildenstern, and Attendants.*

King

Welcome, dear Rosencrantz and Guildenstern!
Moreover that we much did long to see you,
The need we have to use you did provoke
Our hasty sending. Something have you heard

6, 12 **sith:** since.

12 **havior:** behavior.
13 **vouchsafe your rest:** agree to stay.

22 **gentry:** courtesy.

Of Hamlet's transformation; so call it,   5
Sith nor th' exterior nor the inward man
Resembles that it was. What it should be,
More than his father's death, that thus hath put him
So much from th' understanding of himself,
I cannot dream of: I entreat you both,   10
That, being of so young days brought up with him
And sith so neighbor'd to his youth and havior,
That you vouchsafe your rest here in our court
Some little time: so by your companies
To draw him on to pleasures, and to gather   15
So much as from occasion you may glean,
Whether aught to us unknown afflicts him thus,
That open'd lies within our remedy.

Queen
Good gentlemen, he hath much talk'd of you,
And sure I am two men there are not living   20
To whom he more adheres. If it will please you
To show us so much gentry and good will
As to expend your time with us awhile
For the supply and profit of our hope,
Your visitation shall receive such thanks   25
As fits a king's remembrance.

Rosencrantz
                              Both your majesties
Might, by the sovereign power you have of us,
Put your dread pleasures more into command
Than to entreaty.   30

Guildenstern
                      But we both obey,
And here give up ourselves, in the full bent
To lay our service freely at your feet,
To be commanded.

King
Thanks, Rosencrantz and gentle Guildenstern.   35

45 **still:**   always.

46 **liege:**   lord, sovereign.

55 **fruit:**   dessert.

Queen
  Thanks, Guildenstern and gentle Rosencrantz:
  And I beseech you instantly to visit
  My too much changed son. Go, some of you,
  And bring these gentlemen where Hamlet is.

Guildenstern
  Heavens make our presence and our practices   40
  Pleasant and helpful to him!

Queen
                    Aye, amen!
          [*Exeunt Rosencrantz, Guildenstern, and some
                              Attendants.*

          Enter Polonius.

Polonius
  Th' ambassadors from Norway, my good lord,
  Are joyfully return'd.

King
  Thou still hast been the father of good news.   45

Polonius
  Have I, my lord? I assure my good liege,
  I hold my duty as I hold my soul,
  Both to my God and to my gracious king:
  And I do think, or else this brain of mine
  Hunts not the trail of policy so sure   50
  As it hath us'd to do, that I have found
  The very cause of Hamlet's lunacy.

King
  O, speak of that; that do I long to hear.

Polonius
  Give first admittance to th' ambassadors;
  My news shall be the fruit to that great feast.   55

King
  Thyself do grace to them, and bring them in.
                              [*Exit Polonius.*

59 **main:**   chief cause.

61 **sift:**   question.

65 **first:**   first audience.
66 **levies:**   troops.

71 **falsely borne in hand:**   tricked, deceived.

75 **give th' assay of arms against:**   attack.

83 **regards:**   conditions.

He tells me, my dear Gertrude, he hath found
The head and source of all your son's distemper.

Queen
I doubt it is no other but the main;
His father's death and our o'erhasty marriage.   60

King
Well, we shall sift him.

Reenter Polonius, with Voltimand and Cornelius.

Welcome, my good friends!
Say, Voltimand, what from our brother Norway?

Voltimand
Most fair return of greetings and desires.
Upon our first, he sent out to suppress   65
His nephew's levies, which to him appear'd
To be a preparation 'gainst the Polack,
But better look'd into, he truly found
It was against your highness: whereat griev'd,
That so his sickness, age and impotence   70
Was falsely borne in hand, sends out arrests
On Fortinbras; which he, in brief, obeys,
Receives rebuke from Norway, and in fine
Makes vow before his uncle never more
To give th' assay of arms against your majesty.   75
Whereon old Norway, overcome with joy,
Gives him three thousand crowns in annual fee
And his commission to employ those soldiers,
So levied as before, against the Polack:
With an entreaty, herein further shown,   80
                              [*Giving a paper.*
That it might please you to give quiet pass
Through your dominions for this enterprise,
On such regards of safety and allowance
As therein are set down.

King
                    It likes us well,   85

92 **expostulate:** discuss.

105 **figure:** figure of speech.

112 **perpend:** consider.

And at our more consider'd time we'll read,
Answer, and think upon this business.
Meantime we thank you for your well-took labor:
Go to your rest; at night we'll feast together:
Most welcome home!   90

> [*Exeunt Voltimand and Cornelius.*

Polonius

                This business is well ended.
My liege, and madam, to expostulate
What majesty should be, what duty is,
Why day is day, night night, and time is time,
Were nothing but to waste night, day and time.   95
Therefore, since brevity is the soul of wit
And tediousness the limbs and outward flourishes,
I will be brief. Your noble son is mad:
Mad call I it; for, to define true madness,
What is 't but to be nothing else but mad?   100
But let that go.

Queen

                More matter, with less art.

Polonius

Madam, I swear I use no art at all.
That he is mad, 'tis true: 'tis true 'tis pity,
And pity 'tis 'tis true: a foolish figure;   105
But farewell it, for I will use no art.
Mad let us grant him then: and now remains
That we find out the cause of this effect,
Or rather say, the cause of this defect,
For this effect defective comes by cause: 110
Thus it remains and the remainder thus.
Perpend.
I have a daughter—have while she is mine—
Who in her duty and obedience, mark,
Hath given me this: now gather and surmise.   115

> [*Reads.*

"To the celestial, and my soul's idol, the most beauti-

127 **numbers:** verses.
128 **reckon my groans:** count up all my pains for your love.

130 **machine:** body.

fied Ophelia—"
That's an ill phrase, a vile phrase; "beautified" is a
vile phrase; but you shall hear. Thus:

[*Reads.*

"In her excellent white bosom, these," &c.   120
Queen
Came this from Hamlet to her?
Polonius
Good madam, stay awhile; I will be faithful.

[*Reads.*

"Doubt thou the stars are fire;
Doubt that the sun doth move;
Doubt truth to be a liar;   125
But never doubt I love.

"O dear Ophelia, I am ill at these numbers; I have
not art to reckon my groans: but that I love thee
best, O most best, believe it. Adieu. Thine evermore,
most dear lady, whilst this machine is to him,   130
                                             Hamlet."
This in obedience hath my daughter shown me;
And more above, hath his solicitings,
As they fell out by time, by means and place,
All given to mine ear.   135
King
                        But how hath she
Receiv'd his love?
Polonius
                        What do you think of me?
King
As of a man faithful and honorable.
Polonius
I would fain prove so. But what might you think,   140
When I had seen this hot love on the wing—
As I perceiv'd it, I must tell you that,
Before my daughter told me—what might you,

145 **play'd the desk or table-book:** remained silent.

149 **bespeak:** speak to, address.

151 **prescripts:** orders.

157 **watch:** state of sleeplessness.
158 **declension:** decline, deterioration.

Or my dear majesty your queen here, think,
If I had play'd the desk or table-book, 145
Or given my heart a winking, mute and dumb,
Or look'd upon this love with idle sight;
What might you think? No, I went round to work,
And my young mistress thus I did bespeak:
"Lord Hamlet is a prince, out of thy star; 150
This must not be": and then I prescripts gave her,
That she should lock herself from his resort,
Admit no messengers, receive no tokens.
Which done, she took the fruits of my advice;
And he repulsed, a short tale to make, 155
Fell into a sadness, then into a fast,
Thence to a watch, thence into a weakness,
Thence to a lightness, and by this declension
Into the madness wherein now he raves
And all we mourn for. 160

King
Do you think this?

Queen
        It may be, very like.

Polonius
Hath there been such a time, I'd fain know that,
That I have positively said " 'tis so,"
When it prov'd otherwise? 165

King
        Not that I know.

Polonius
  [*Pointing to his head and shoulder*]
Take this from this, if this be otherwise:
If circumstances lead me, I will find
Where truth is hid, though it were hid indeed
Within the center. 170

King
        How may we try it further?

176 **arras:**   tapestry.

180 **carters:**   carts.

184 **board:**   address.

188 **fishmonger:**   one who sells fish.

Polonius
    You know, sometimes he walks four hours together
    Here in the lobby.
Queen
                        So he does, indeed.
Polonius
    At such a time I'll loose my daughter to him: 175
    Be you and I behind an arras then;
    Mark the encounter: if he love her not,
    And be not from his reason fall'n thereon,
    Let me be no assistant for a state,
    But keep a farm and carters.   180
King
                        We will try it.
Queen
    But look where sadly the poor wretch comes reading.
Polonius
    Away, I do beseech you, both away:
    I'll board him presently.
                    [*Exeunt King, Queen, and Attendants.*

    Enter Hamlet, reading.

    O, give me leave: how does my good Lord Hamlet?   185
Hamlet
    Well, God-a-mercy.
Polonius
    Do you know me, my lord?
Hamlet
    Excellent well; you are a fishmonger.
Polonius
    Not I, my lord.
Hamlet
    Then I would you were so honest a man.   190
Polonius
    Honest, my lord.

196 **god kissing carrion:**   sun god pouring his rays upon dead flesh.

214 **honesty:**   honorable behavior.

Hamlet

Aye, sir; to be honest, as this world goes, is to be one
man picked out of ten thousand.

Polonius

That's very true, my lord.

Hamlet

For if the sun breed maggots in a dead dog, being　195
a god kissing carrion—Have you a daughter?

Polonius

I have, my lord.

Hamlet

Let her not walk i' the sun: conception is a blessing;
but as your daughter may conceive—friend, look to 't.

Polonius

[*Aside*]　How say you by that? Still harping on my　200
daughter: yet he knew me not at first: he said I was
a fishmonger: he is far gone: and truly in my youth
I suffered much extremity for love; very near this.
I'll speak to him again.—What do you read, my lord?

Hamlet

Words, words, words.　205

Polonius

What is the matter, my lord?

Hamlet

Between who?

Polonius

I mean, the matter that you read, my lord.

Hamlet

Slanders, sir: for the satirical rogue says here that old
men have gray beards, that their faces are wrinkled,　210
their eyes purging thick amber and plum-tree gum,
and that they have a plentiful lack of wit, together
with most weak hams: all which, sir, though I most
powerfully and potently believe, yet I hold it not honesty to have it thus set down; for yourself, sir, shall　215
grow old as I am, if like a crab you could go backward.

220 **pregnant:**   meaningful.
221 **happiness:**   happy phrase, aptness of expression.

228 **withal:**   with.

Polonius
  [Aside] Though this be madness, yet there is method
  in 't.—Will you walk out of the air, my lord?
Hamlet
  Into my grave.
Polonius
  Indeed, that's out of the air. [Aside] How pregnant   220
  sometimes his replies are! a happiness that often mad-
  ness hits on, which reason and sanity could not so
  prosperously be delivered of. I will leave him, and sud-
  denly contrive the means of meeting between him
  and my daughter.—My honorable lord, I will most   225
  humbly take my leave of you.
Hamlet
  You cannot, sir, take from me any thing that I will
  more willingly part withal: except my life, except my
  life, except my life.
Polonius
  Fare you well, my lord.   230
Hamlet
  These tedious old fools.

        Reenter Rosencrantz and Guildenstern.

Polonius
  You go to seek the Lord Hamlet; there he is.
Rosencrantz
  [To Polonius]   God save you, sir!
                                              [Exit Polonius.
Guildenstern
  My honor'd lord!
Rosencrantz
  My most dear lord!   235
Hamlet
  My excellent good friends! How dost thou, Guilden-
  stern? Ah, Rosencrantz! Good lads, how do you both?

238 **indifferent:** average, ordinary.

256 **confines:** places of confinement.

Rosencrantz
  As the indifferent children of the earth.

Guildenstern
  Happy, in that we are not over-happy;
  On Fortune's cap we are not the very button. 240

Hamlet
  Nor the soles of her shoe?

Rosencrantz
  Neither, my lord.

Hamlet
  Then you live about her waist, or in the middle of
  her favors?

Guildenstern
  Faith, her privates we. 245

Hamlet
  In the secret parts of Fortune? O, most true; she is
  a strumpet. What's the news?

Rosencrantz
  None, my lord, but that the world's grown honest.

Hamlet
  Then is doomsday near: but your news is not true.
  Let me question more in particular: what have you, 250
  my good friends, deserved at the hands of Fortune,
  that she sends you to prison hither?

Guildenstern
  Prison, my lord!

Hamlet
  Denmark's a prison.

Rosencrantz
  Then is the world one. 255

Hamlet
  A goodly one; in which there are many confines,
  wards and dungeons, Denmark being one o' the worst.

275 **fay:** faith.

276 **wait upon:** accompany. (Hamlet jocularly accepts the phase literally.)

Rosencrantz
We think not so, my lord.

Hamlet
Why, then, 'tis none to you; for there is nothing
either good or bad, but thinking makes it so: to me   260
it is a prison.

Rosencrantz
Why, then your ambition makes it one; 'tis too nar-
row for your mind.

Hamlet
O God, I could be bounded in a nutshell and count
myself a king of infinite space, were it not that I have   265
bad dreams.

Guildenstern
Which dreams indeed are ambition; for the very substance of the ambitious is merely the shadow of a
dream.

Hamlet
A dream itself is but a shadow.   270

Rosencrantz
Truly, and I hold ambition of so airy and light a
quality that it is but a shadow's shadow.

Hamlet
Then are our beggars bodies, and our monarchs and
outstretched heroes the beggars' shadows. Shall we to
the court? for, by my fay, I cannot reason.   275

Rosencrantz and Guildenstern
We'll wait upon you.

Hamlet
No such matter: I will not sort you with the rest of
my servants; for, to speak to you like an honest man,
I am most dreadfully attended. But, in the beaten
way of friendship, what make you at Elsinore?   280

Rosencrantz
To visit you, my lord; no other occasion.

290 **color:** disguise.

293 **conjure:** urge.

294–295 **consonancy of our youth:** boyhood friendship.

303–304 **prevent your discovery:** precede your disclosure.

305 **moult no feather:** be undamaged.

Hamlet

Beggar that I am, I am even poor in thanks; but I
thank you: and sure, dear friends, my thanks are too
dear a halfpenny. Were you not sent for? Is it your
own inclining? Is it a free visitation? Come, deal justly   285
with me: come, come; nay, speak.

Guildenstern

What should we say, my lord?

Hamlet

Why, any thing, but to the purpose. You were sent
for; and there is a kind of confession in your looks,
which your modesties have not craft enough to color: 290
I know the good king and queen have sent for you.

Rosencrantz

To what end, my lord?

Hamlet

That you must teach me. But let me conjure you, by
the rights of our fellowship, by the consonancy of
our youth, by the obligation of our ever-preserved   295
love, and by what more dear a better proposer could
charge you withal, be even and direct with me,
whether you were sent for, or no.

Rosencrantz

[*Aside to Guildenstern*]   What say you?

Hamlet

[*Aside*]   Nay then, I have an eye of you.—   300
If you love me, hold not off.

Guildenstern

My lord, we were sent for.

Hamlet

I will tell you why; so shall my anticipation prevent
your discovery, and your secrecy to the king and
queen moult no feather. I have of late—but wherefore   305
I know not—lost all my mirth, forgone all custom
of exercises; and indeed it goes so heavily with my

311 **fretted:** adorned with carving.

315 **faculty:** ability.
   express: expressive, perfect.
316 **apprehension:** perception.

319 **quintessence:** highest quality.

326 **lenten:** meager.
327 **coted:** overtook.

331 **target:** shield.

334 **tickle o' the sere:** easily moved to laughter.

disposition that this goodly frame, the earth, seen
to me a sterile promontory; this most excellent can-
opy, the air, look you, this brave o'erhanging firma-   310
ment, this majestical roof fretted with golden fire,
why, it appears no other thing to me than a foul
and pestilent congregation of vapors. What a piece
of work is a man! how noble in reason! how infinite in faculty! in form and moving how express   315
and admirable! in action how like an angel! in apprehension how like a god! the beauty of the world! the
paragon of animals! And yet, to me, what is this
quintessence of dust? man delights not me; no, nor
woman neither, though by your smiling you seem to   320
say so.

Rosencrantz
My lord, there was no such stuff in my thoughts.

Hamlet
Why did you laugh then, when I said "man delights
not me"?

Rosencrantz
To think, my lord, if you delight not in man, what   325
lenten entertainment the players shall receive from
you: we coted them on the way; and hither are they
coming, to offer you service.

Hamlet
He that plays the king shall be welcome; his majesty
shall have tribute of me; the adventurous knight   330
shall use his foil and target; the lover shall not sigh
gratis; the humorous man shall end his part in peace;
the clown shall make those laugh whose lungs are
tickle o' the sere, and the lady shall say her mind
freely, or the blank verse shall halt for 't. What   335
players are they?

Rosencrantz
Even those you were wont to take such delight in,
the tragedians of the city.

341 **inhibition:** prohibition.
342 **late innovation:** recent change.

347 **wonted:** usual.
348 **eyrie:** nest.
     eyases: young hawks.
350 **clapped:** applauded.
351 **berattle:** make fun of.
     the common stages: the public theater.

357 **common:** regular, ordinary.

362 **tarre:** incite.

364 **went to cuffs:** came to blows.

Hamlet

How chances it they travel? their residence, both in
reputation and profit, was better both ways.   340

Rosencrantz

I think their inhibition comes by the means of the
late innovation.

Hamlet

Do they hold the same estimation they did when I
was in the city? are they so follow'd?

Rosencrantz

No, indeed, are they not.   345

Hamlet

How comes it? do they grow rusty?

Rosencrantz

Nay, their endeavor keeps in the wonted pace: but
there is, sir, an eyrie of children, little eyases, that cry
out on the top of question and are most tyrannically
clapped for 't: these are now the fashion, and so   350
berattle the common stages—so they call them—that
many wearing rapiers are afraid of goose-quills, and
dare scarce come thither.

Hamlet

What, are they children? who maintains 'em? how
are they escorted? Will they pursue the quality no   355
longer than they can sing? will they not say after-
wards, if they should grow themselves to common
players—as it is most like, if their means are no better—their writers do them wrong, to make them
exclaim against their own succession?   360

Rosencrantz

Faith, there has been much to do on both sides, and
the nation holds it no sin to tarre them to contro-
versy: there was for a while no money bid for argument unless the poet and the player went to cuffs in
the question.   365

369 **Hercules and his load:** Hercules and the globe (a symbol of Shakespeare's own playhouse, the Globe).

371 **mows:** grimaces.

373 **little:** miniature.
   'Sblood: God's blood (an oath).

378 **appurtenance:** proper accompaniment.
379 **garb:** fashion, manner.
380 **extent:** behavior.

Hamlet

Is 't possible?

Guildenstern

O, there has been much throwing about of brains.

Hamlet

Do the boys carry it away?

Rosencrantz

Aye, that they do, my lord; Hercules and his load too.

Hamlet

It is not very strange; for my uncle is king of Den-　370
mark, and those that would make mows at him while
my father lived, give twenty, forty, fifty, a hundred
ducats apiece, for his picture in little. 'Sblood, there
is something in this more than natural, if philosophy
could find it out.　　　　　　　　　　　　　　　　375

　　　　　　　　　　[*Flourish of trumpets within.*

Guildenstern

There are the players.

Hamlet

Gentlemen, you are welcome to Elsinore. Your hands,
come then: the appurtenance of welcome is fashion
and ceremony: let me comply with you in this garb,
lest my extent to the players, which, I tell you, must　380
show fairly outwards, should more appear like entertainment than yours. You are welcome: but my
uncle-father and aunt-mother are deceived.

Guildenstern

In what, my dear lord?

Hamlet

I am but mad north-north-west: when the wind is　385
southerly I know a hawk from a handsaw.

　　Reenter Polonius.

Polonius

Well be with you, gentlemen!

390 **swaddling clouts:**   baby clothes.

391 **Happily:**   perhaps.

406 **individable:**   a play in which the unity of place is pre-
serveded.
poem unlimited: a play in which the unity is not observed.
406–407 **Seneca and Plautus:**   Roman writers of comedies.
407–408 **law of writ and the liberty:**   observing rules or disre-
garding them.
409 **Jephthah:**   In the Bible, Jephthah promised to sacrifice the
first creature he met on his return home from a successful
expedition. It turned out to be his daughter.

Hamlet

Hark you, Guildenstern; and you too: at each ear
a hearer: that great baby you see there is not yet
out of his swaddling clouts.   390

Rosencrantz

Happily he's the second time come to them; for they
say an old man is twice a child.

Hamlet

I will prophesy he comes to tell me of the players;
mark it. You say right, sir: o' Monday morning;
'twas so, indeed.   395

Polonius

My lord, I have news to tell you.

Hamlet

My lord, I have news to tell you. When Roscius
was an actor in Rome—

Polonius

The actors are come hither, my lord.

Hamlet

Buz, buz!   400

Polonius

Upon my honor—

Hamlet

Then came each actor on his ass—

Polonius

The best actors in the world, either for tragedy,
comedy, history, pastoral, pastoral-comical, historical-
pastoral, tragical-historical, tragical-comical-historical-   405
pastoral, scene individable, or poem unlimited: Seneca
cannot be too heavy, nor Plautus too light. For the law
of writ and the liberty, these are the only men.

Hamlet

O Jephthah, judge of Israel, what a treasure hadst
thou!   410

425 **row:** stanza.
chanson: song.
426 **abridgment:** entertainment for pastime.

429 **valanced:** bearded.

431 **young lady and mistress:** actually, of course, a young boy who plays women's roles.
433 **chopine:** high cork shoe.
434–435 **cracked within the ring:** If the outer ring of a gold coin was cracked, it could no longer circulate. Hamlet hopes the boy's voice has not changed.

Polonius
What a treasure had he, my lord?

Hamlet
Why,
      "One fair daughter, and no more,
        The which he loved passing well."

Polonius
[*Aside*]   Still on my daughter.   415

Hamlet
Am I not i' the right, old Jephthah?

Polonius
If you call me Jephthah, my lord, I have a daughter
that I love passing well.

Hamlet
Nay, that follows not.

Polonius
What follows, then, my lord?   420

Hamlet
Why,

            "As by lot, God wot,"
and then you know,

      "It came to pass, as most like it was"—
the first row of the pious chanson will show you   425
more; for look, where my abridgment comes.

      Enter four or five Players.

You are welcome, masters; welcome, all. I am glad
to see thee well. Welcome, good friends. O, my old
friend! Why thy face is valanced since I saw thee
last; comest thou to beard me in Denmark? What,   430
my young lady and mistress! By'r lady, your lady-
ship is nearer to heaven than when I saw you last,
by the altitude of a chopine. Pray God, your voice,
like a piece of uncurrent gold, be not cracked within
the ring. Masters, you are all welcome. We'll e'en   435

442–443 **caviare to the general:** too good for the common people.

444 **cried in the top of:** exceeded.

446 **modesty:** moderation.

447 **sallets:** relish, hence spicy quips.

452 **Æneas:** Trojan who was the legendary founder of Rome.

453 **Dido:** The *Æneid* tells of Dido's hopeless love for Æneas, who stayed for a while at Carthage after leaving Troy.

454 **Priam:** King of Troy, killed during the fall of Troy.

456 **Pyrrhus:** son of Achilles, slayer of Priam.
Hyrcanian beast: tiger.

460 **ominous horse:** the gigantic Trojan Horse.

463 **gules:** red—a term in heraldry.
trick'd: adorned—a term in heraldry.

465 **impasted:** made into paste.

468 **o'ersized:** covered as with glue.
coagulate gore: blood that has thickened.

469 **carbuncles:** boils.

to 't like French falconers, fly at any thing we see:
we'll have a speech straight: come, give us a taste of
your quality; come, a passionate speech.

First Player
What speech, my good lord?

Hamlet
I heard thee speak me a speech once, but it was never   440
acted; or, if it was, not above once; for the play, I
remember, pleased not the million; 'twas caviare to
the general: but it was—as I received it, and others,
whose judgments in such matters cried in the top of
mine—an excellent play, well digested in the scenes,   445
set down with as much modesty as cunning. I remember, one said there were no sallets in the lines
to make the matter savory, nor no matter in the
phrase that might indict the author of affection; but
called it an honest method, as wholesome as sweet,   450
and by very much more handsome than fine. One
speech in it I chiefly loved: 'twas Æneas' tale to
Dido; and thereabout of it especially, where he speaks
of Priam's slaughter: if it live in your memory, begin
at this line; let me see, let me see;   455
"The rugged Pyrrhus, like th' Hyrcanian beast"—
It is not so: it begins with "Pyrrhus."
"The rugged Pyrrhus, he whose sable arms,
Black as his purpose, did the night resemble
When he lay couched in the ominous horse,   460
Hath now this dread and black complexion smear'd
With heraldry more dismal: head to foot
Now is he total gules; horridly trick'd
With the blood of fathers, mothers, daughters, sons,
Bak'd and impasted with the parching streets   465
That lend a tyrannous and a damned light
To their lord's murder: roasted in wrath and fire,
And thus o'ersized with coagulate gore,
With eyes like carbuncles, the hellish Pyrrhus

480 **Ilium:** Troy.

489 **against:** before.
490 **rack:** mass of clouds.

493 **rend the region:** shatter the upper air.

495 **Cyclops:** one of the legendary giants who assisted Vulcan, god of fire, in his blacksmith shop.
496 **Mars:** god of war.
    proof eterne: eternal trial.

500 **synod:** assembly.
501 **fellies:** wheel rims.
502 **nave:** hub.

Old grandsire Priam seeks." 470
So, proceed you.

Polonius
'Fore God, my lord, well spoken, with good accent
and good discretion.

First Player
           "Anon he finds him
Striking too short at Greeks; his antique sword, 475
Rebellious to his arm, lies where it falls,
Repugnant to command: unequal match'd,
Pyrrhus at Priam drives; in rage strikes wide;
But with the whiff and wind of his fell sword
Th' unnerved father falls. Then senseless Ilium, 480
Seeming to feel this blow, with flaming top
Stoops to his base, and with a hideous crash
Takes prisoner Pyrrhus' ear: for, lo! his sword,
Which was declining on the milky head
Of reverend Priam, seem'd i' th' air to stick: 485
So, as a painted tyrant, Pyrrhus stood,
And like a neutral to his will and matter,
Did nothing.
But as we often see, against some storm,
A silence in the heavens, the rack stand still, 490
The bold winds speechless and the orb below
As hush as death, anon the dreadful thunder
Doth rend the region, so after Pyrrhus' pause
Aroused vengeance sets him new a-work;
And never did the Cyclops' hammers fall 495
On Mars's armor, forg'd for proof eterne,
With less remorse than Pyrrhus' bleeding sword
Now falls on Priam.
Out, out, thou strumpet, Fortune! All you gods,
In general synod take away her power, 500
Break all the spokes and fellies from her wheel,
And bowl the round nave down the hill of heaven
As low as to the fiends!"

508 **mobled:**   muffled.
   queen: Hecuba, Queen of Troy, wife of Priam.

512 **bisson rheum:**   blinding tears.

514 **o'er-teemed:**   worn out with child bearing.

523 **milch:**   milk-giving, hence moist.

Polonius
This is too long.

Hamlet
It shall to the barber's, with your beard.   505
Prithee, say on: he's for a jig or a tale of bawdry, or
he sleeps: say on: come to Hecuba.

First Player
"But who, O, who had seen the mobled queen—"

Hamlet
"The mobled queen?"

Polonius
That's good; "mobled queen" is good.   510

First Player
"Run barefoot up and down, threat'ning the flames
With bisson rheum; a clout upon that head
Where late the diadem stood; and for a robe,
About her lank and all o'er-teemed loins,
A blanket, in the alarm of fear caught up: 515
Who this had seen, with tongue in venom steep'd
'Gainst Fortune's state would treason have pronounc'd:
But if the gods themselves did see her then,
When she saw Pyrrhus make malicious sport
In mincing with his sword her husband's limbs,   520
The instant burst of clamor that she made,
Unless things mortal move them not at all,
Would have made milch the burning eyes of heaven
And passion in the gods."

Polonius
Look, whether he has not turned his color and has   525
tears in 's eyes. Prithee, no more.

Hamlet
'Tis well; I'll have thee speak out the rest of this
soon. Good my lord, will you see the players well
bestowed? Do you hear, let them be well used, for
they are the abstract and brief chronicles of the time: 530

534 **God's bodykins:**   by God's body (an oath).

544 **ha 't:**   have it.

after your death you were better have a bad epitaph
than their ill report while you live.

Polonius

My lord, I will use them according to their desert.

Hamlet

God's bodykins, man, much better: use every man
after his desert, and who shall 'scape whipping? Use   535
them after your own honor and dignity: the less they
deserve, the more merit is in your bounty. Take them
in.

Polonius

Come, sirs.

Hamlet

Follow him, friends: we'll hear a play tomorrow.   540
    [*Exit Polonius with all the Players but the First.*
Dost thou hear me, old friend; can you play the
Murder of Gonzago?

First Player

Aye, my lord.

Hamlet

We'll ha 't tomorrow night. You could, for a need,
study a speech of some dozen or sixteen lines, which   545
I would set down and insert in 't, could you not?

First Player

Aye, my lord.

Hamlet

Very well. Follow that lord; and look you mock him
not.
                    [*Exit First Player.*
My good friends, I'll leave you till night: you are   550
welcome to Elsinore.

Rosencrantz

Good my lord!

Hamlet

Aye, so, God be wi' ye!

558 **conceit:** imagination.
559 **visage wann'd:** blood drained from his face.
560 **distraction:** extreme upset.

573 **muddy-mettled:** dull spirited, irresolute.
    peak: play a contemptible part.
574 **John-a-dreams:** a dreamer.
    unpregnant of: indifferent to.

578 **pate:** head.

583 **'Swounds:** God's wounds (an oath).
584 **pigeon-liver'd:** cowardly.

586 **kites:** scavenger birds.
587 **this slave's offal:** King Claudius's guts.

[*Exeunt Rosencrantz and Guildenster*
Now I am alone.
O, what a rogue and peasant slave am I!   555
Is it not monstrous that this player here,
But in a fiction, in a dream of passion,
Could force his soul so to his own conceit
That from her working all his visage wann'd;
Tears in his eyes, distraction in 's aspect,   560
A broken voice, and his whole function suiting
With forms to his conceit? and all for nothing!
For Hecuba!
What's Hecuba to him, or he to Hecuba,
That he should weep for her? What would he do,   565
Had he the motive and the cue for passion
That I have? He would drown the stage with tears
And cleave the general air with horrid speech,
Make mad the guilty and appal the free,
Confound the ignorant, and amaze indeed   570
The very faculties of eyes and ears.
Yet I,
A dull and muddy-mettled rascal, peak,
Like John-a-dreams, unpregnant of my cause,
And can say nothing; no, not for a king,   575
Upon whose property and most dear life
A damn'd defeat was made. Am I a coward?
Who calls me villain? breaks my pate across?
Plucks off my beard, and blows it in my face?
Tweaks me by the nose? gives me the lie i' the throat,   580
As deep as to the lungs? who does me this?
Ha!
'Swounds, I should take it: for it cannot be
But I am pigeon-liver'd and lack gall
To make oppression bitter, or ere this   585
I should have fatted all the region kites
With this slave's offal: bloody, bawdy villain!
Remorseless, treacherous, lecherous, kindless villain!

594 **drab:** prostitute.
595 **scullion:** kitchen servant.

599 **presently:** immediately.
600 **malefactions:** evil actions.

605 **tent:** probe.
    blench: start aside.

611 **abuses:** deceives.

O, vengeance!
Why, what an ass am I! This is most brave,　　　590
That I, the son of a dear father murder'd,
Prompted to my revenge by heaven and hell,
Must, like a whore, unpack my heart with words,
And fall a-cursing, like a very drab,
A scullion!　　　595
Fie upon 't! foh! About, my brain! Hum, I have
　　heard
That guilty creatures, sitting at a play,
Have by the very cunning of the scene
Been struck so to the soul that presently
They have proclaim'd their malefactions;　　　600
For murder, though it have no tongue, will speak
With most miraculous organ. I'll have these players
Play something like the murder of my father
Before mine uncle: I'll observe his looks;
I'll tent him to the quick: if he but blench,　　　605
I know my course. The spirit that I have seen
May be the devil; and the devil hath power
To assume a pleasing shape; yea, and perhaps
Out of my weakness and my melancholy,
As he is very potent with such spirits,　　　610
Abuses me to damn me. I'll have grounds
More relative than this. The play's the thing
Wherein I'll catch the conscience of the king.
　　　　　　　　　　　　[*Exit.*

1 **drift of circumstance:**   turn of conversation.

7 **forward:**   disposed.

13 **forcing of his disposition:**   reluctant courtesy.

14 **niggard of question:**   sparing in his talk.

16 **assay:**   try.

ACT III

Scene 1. *A room in the castle*

Enter King, Queen, Polonius, Ophelia, Rosencrantz,
and Guildenstern.

King
And can you, by no drift of circumstance,
Get from him why he puts on this confusion,
Grating so harshly all his days of quiet
With turbulent and dangerous lunacy?

Rosencrantz
He does confess he feels himself distracted,   5
But from what cause he will by no means speak.

Guildenstern
Nor do we find him forward to be sounded;
But, with a crafty madness, keeps aloof,
When we would bring him on to some confession
Of his true state.   10

Queen
                    Did he receive you well?

Rosencrantz
Most like a gentleman.

Guildenstern
But with much forcing of his disposition.

Rosencrantz
Niggard of question, but of our demands
Most free in his reply.   15

Queen
                    Did you assay him
To any pastime?

19 **o'er-raught:**   overtook.

29 **edge:**   incitement, encouragement.

33 **closely:**   secretly.

35 **affront:**   confront, encounter.
36 **espials:**   spies.

Rosencrantz
 Madam, it so fell out that certain players
 We o'er-raught on the way: of these we told him,
 And there did seem in him a kind of joy   20
 To hear of it: they are about the court,
 And, as I think, they have already order
 This night to play before him.

Polonius
        'Tis most true:
 And he beseech'd me to entreat your majesties 25
 To hear and see the matter.

King
 With all my heart; and it doth much content me
 To hear him so inclin'd.
 Good gentlemen, give him a further edge,
 And drive his purpose on to these delights.   30

Rosencrantz
 We shall, my lord.
    [*Exeunt Rosencrantz and Guildenstern.*

King
      Sweet Gertrude, leave us too;
 For we have closely sent for Hamlet hither,
 That he, as 'twere by accident, may here
 Affront Ophelia: 35
 Her father and myself, lawful espials,
 Will so bestow ourselves that, seeing unseen,
 We may of their encounter frankly judge,
 And gather by him, as he is behav'd,
 If 't be th' affliction of his love or no   40
 That thus he suffers for.

Queen
      I shall obey you:
 And for your part, Ophelia, I do wish
 That your good beauties be the happy cause
 Of Hamlet's wildness: so shall I hope your virtues 45

60 **to:** compared to.

62 **burthen:** burden.

Will bring him to his wonted way again,
To both your honors.

Ophelia

　　　　　　Madam, I wish it may.

　　　　　　　　　　　　　[Exit Queen.

Polonius

Ophelia, walk you here. Gracious, so please you,
We will bestow ourselves.   50
　　[To Ophelia.]　　　　　Read on this book;
That show of such an exercise may color
Your loneliness. We are oft to blame in this—
'Tis too much prov'd—that with devotion's visage
And pious action we do sugar o'er   55
The devil himself.

King

　　[Aside]　　　　O, 'tis too true!
How smart a lash that speech doth give my
　　　　conscience!
The harlot's cheek, beautied with plast'ring art,
Is not more ugly to the thing that helps it   60
Than is my deed to my most painted word:
O heavy burthen!

Polonius

I hear him coming: let's withdraw, my lord.
　　　　　　　　[Exeunt King and Polonius.

　　Enter Hamlet.

Hamlet

To be, or not to be: that is the question:
Whether 'tis nobler in the mind to suffer   65
The slings and arrows of outrageous fortune,
Or to take arms against a sea of troubles,
And by opposing end them. To die: to sleep;
No more; and by a sleep to say we end
The heart-ache, and the thousand natural shocks   70
That flesh is heir to, 'tis a consummation

75 **mortal coil:** mortal life.

79 **contumely:** rudeness, insolence.

83 **quietus:** settlement (a legal term).
84 **bodkin:** dagger.
   fardels: packs, burdens.

87 **bourn:** limit, boundary.

91 **conscience:** thinking.

94 **pitch:** importance.

97 **Nymph:** beautiful young lady.
   orisons: prayers.

Devoutly to be wish'd. To die, to sleep;
To sleep: perchance to dream: aye, there's the rub;
For in that sleep of death what dreams may come,
When we have shuffled off this mortal coil,   75
Must give us pause: there's the respect
That makes calamity of so long life;
For who would bear the whips and scorns of time,
Th' oppressor's wrong, the proud man's contumely,
The pangs of despis'd love, the law's delay,   80
The insolence of office, and the spurns
That patient merit of th' unworthy takes,
When he himself might his quietus make
With a bare bodkin? who would fardels bear,
To grunt and sweat under a weary life,   85
But that the dread of something after death,
The undiscover'd country from whose bourn
No traveler returns, puzzles the will,
And makes us rather bear those ills we have
Than fly to others that we know not of?   90
‐Thus conscience does make cowards of us all,
And thus the native hue of resolution
Is sicklied o'er with the pale cast of thought,
And enterprises of great pitch and moment
With this regard their currents turn awry   95
And lose the name of action. Soft you now!
The fair Ophelia! Nymph, in thy orisons
Be all my sins remember'd.

Ophelia
                         Good my lord,
How does your honor for this many a day?   100

Hamlet
    I humbly thank you: well, well, well.

Ophelia
    My lord, I have remembrances of yours,
    That I have longed to redeliver;
    I pray you, now receive them.

111 **wax poor:**   become poor.

113 **honest:**   virtuous.

124 **sometime:**   formerly.

Hamlet

No, not I;   105

I never gave you aught.

Ophelia

My honor'd lord, you know right well you did;
And with them words of so sweet breath compos'd
As made the things more rich: their perfume lost,
Take these again; for to the noble mind   110
Rich gifts wax poor when givers prove unkind
There, my lord.

Hamlet

Ha, ha! are you honest?

Ophelia

My lord?

Hamlet

Are you fair?   115

Ophelia

What means your lordship?

Hamlet

That if you be honest and fair, your honesty should
admit no discourse to your beauty.

Ophelia

Could beauty, my lord, have better commerce than
with honesty?   120

Hamlet

Aye, truly; for the power of beauty will sooner trans-
form honesty from what it is to a bawd than the
force of honesty can translate beauty into his likeness:
this was sometime a paradox, but now the time gives
it proof. I did love you once.   125

Ophelia

Indeed, my lord, you made me believe so.

Hamlet

You should not have believed me; for virtue cannot

128 **inoculate:**   be grafted on.
     relish of: have a taste, flavor.

136 **beck:**   summoning.

139 **arrant:**   thoroughgoing.

so inoculate our old stock, but we shall relish of it:
I loved you not.

Ophelia

I was the more deceived.   130

Hamlet

Get thee to a nunnery: why wouldst thou be a
breeder of sinners? I am myself indifferent honest;
but yet I could accuse me of such things that it were
better my mother had not borne me: I am very
proud, revengeful, ambitious; with more offenses at   135
my beck than I have thoughts to put them in, imagination to give them shape, or time to act them in.
What should such fellows as I do crawling between
heaven and earth! We are arrant knaves all; believe
none of us. Go thy ways to a nunnery. Where's your   140
father?

Ophelia

At home, my lord.

Hamlet

Let the doors be shut upon him, that he may play
the fool nowhere but in 's own house. Farewell.

Ophelia

O, help him, you sweet heavens!   145

Hamlet

If thou dost marry, I'll give thee this plague for thy
dowry: be thou as chaste as ice, as pure as snow,
thou shalt not escape calumny. Get thee to a nunnery, go: farewell. Or, if thou wilt needs marry, marry
a fool; for wise men know well enough what monsters   150
you make of them. To a nunnery, go; and quickly
too. Farewell.

Ophelia

O heavenly powers, restore him!

Hamlet

I have heard of your paintings too, well enough; God
hath given you one face, and you make yourselves   155

157–158 **make your wantonness your ignorance:** excuse your
willfullness by pleading ignorance.

171 **blown:** full-blown, in its bloom.
172 **blasted with ecstasy:** destroyed by madness.

174 **affections:** feelings.

178 **doubt:** suspect, fear.

another: you jig, you amble, and you lisp, and nick-
name God's creatures, and make your wantonness
your ignorance. Go to, I'll no more on 't; it hath
made me mad. I say, we will have no more marriages:
those that are married already, all but one, shall live;   160
the rest shall keep as they are. To a nunnery, go.
                                                    [*Exit.*

Ophelia
O, what a noble mind is here o'erthrown!
The courtier's, soldier's, scholar's, eye, tongue, sword:
Th' expectancy and rose of the fair state,
The glass of fashion and the mould of form,   165
Th' observ'd of all observers, quite, quite down!
And I, of ladies most deject and wretched,
That suck'd the honey of his music vows,
Now see that noble and most sovereign reason,
Like sweet bells jangled, out of tune and harsh;   170
That unmatch'd form and feature of blown youth
Blasted with ecstasy: O, woe is me,
To have seen what I have seen, see what I see!

        Reenter King and Polonius.

King
Love! his affections do not that way tend;
Nor what he spake, though it lack'd form a little,   175
Was not like madness. There's something in his soul
O'er which his melancholy sits on brood,
And I do doubt the hatch and the disclose
Will be some danger: which for to prevent,
I have in quick determination   180
Thus set it down: he shall with speed to England,
For the demand of our neglected tribute:
Haply the seas and countries different
With variable objects shall expel
This something-settled matter in his heart,   185
Whereon his brains still beating puts him thus
From fashion of himself. What think you on 't?

195 **round:** blunt, outspoken.
196 **in the ear :** listening in .

9 **periwig-pated:** wearing a wig.

11 **groundlings:** crowd who stood in the pit of the theater.

Polonius
　It shall do well: but yet do I believe
　The origin and commencement of his grief
　Sprung from neglected love. How now, Ophelia!　190
　You need not tell us what Lord Hamlet said;
　We heard it all. My lord, do as you please;
　But, if you hold it fit, after the play,
　Let his queen mother all alone entreat him
　To show his grief: let her be round with him;　195
　And I'll be plac'd, so please you, in the ear
　Of all their conference. If she find him not,
　To England send him, or confine him where
　Your wisdom best shall think.

King
　　　　　　　　　It shall be so:　200
　Madness in great ones must not unwatch'd go.
　　　　　　　　　　　　[*Exeunt.*

Scene 2. A hall in the castle

Enter Hamlet and Players.

Hamlet
　Speak the speech, I pray you, as I pronounced it to
you, trippingly on the tongue; but if you mouth it,
as many of your players do, I had as lief the town-
crier spoke my lines. Nor do not saw the air too much
with your hand, thus; but use all gently: for in the　5
very torrent, tempest, and, as I may say, whirlwind
of your passion, you must acquire and beget a temper-
ance that may give it smoothness. O, it offends me
to the soul to hear a robustious periwig-pated fellow
tear a passion to tatters, to very rags, to split the ears　10
of the groundlings, who, for the most part, are ca-

12 **dumb-shows:**   pantomime.

14 **Termagant:**   character in the mystery plays noted for his violent reactions.
Herod: another character noted for his melodramatic acting.
16 **warrant:**   assure.

20 **modesty:**   moderation.

26 **come tardy off:**   being too feebly shown.

34 **journeymen:**   apprentices, assistants.

37 **indifferently:**   pretty well.

42 **barren:**   barren of wit, foolish.

pable of nothing but inexplicable dumb-shows and
noise: I would have such a fellow whipped for o'er-
doing Termagant; it out-herods Herod: pray you,
avoid it.   15

First Player
I warrant your honor.

Hamlet
Be not too tame neither, but let your own discretion
be your tutor: suit the action to the word, the word
to the action; with this special observance, that you
o'erstep not the modesty of nature: for anything so   20
overdone is from the purpose of playing, whose end,
both at the first and now, was and is, to hold, as
'twere, the mirror up to nature; to show virtue her
own feature, scorn her own image, and the very age
and body of the time his form and pressure. Now this   25
overdone or come tardy off, though it make the un-
skillful laugh, cannot but make the judicious grieve;
the censure of the which one must in your allowance
o'erweigh a whole theater of others. O, there be players that I have seen play, and heard others praise,   30
and that highly, not to speak it profanely, that neither
having the accent of Christians nor the gait of Christian, pagan, nor man, have so strutted and bellowed,
that I have thought some of nature's journeymen had
made men, and not made them well, they imitated   35
humanity so abominably.

First Player
I hope we have reformed that indifferently with us,
sir.

Hamlet
O, reform it altogether. And let those that play your
clowns speak no more than is set down for them: 40
for there be of them that will themselves laugh, to set
on some quantity of barren spectators to laugh too,
though in the mean time some necessary question of

56 **as e'er my conversation cop'd withal:** as I've ever met.

62 **candied:** flattering.
63 **crook the pregnant hinges of the knee:** bow and kneel in hope of gaining favor.

the play be then to be considered: that's villainous,
and shows a most pitiful ambition in the fool that   45
uses it. Go, make you ready.

> [*Exeunt Players.*

Enter Polonius, Rosencrantz, and Guildenstern.

How now, my lord! will the king hear this piece of
work?

Polonius
And the queen too, and that presently.

Hamlet
Bid the players make haste.   50

> [*Exit Polonius.*

Will you two help to hasten them?

Rosencrantz and Guildenstern
We will, my lord.

> [*Exeunt Rosencrantz and Guildenstern.*

Hamlet
What ho! Horatio!

Enter Horatio.

Horatio
Here, sweet lord, at your service.

Hamlet
Horatio, thou art e'en as just a man   55
As e'er my conversation cop'd withal.

Horatio
O, my dear lord—

Hamlet
Nay, do not think I flatter;
For what advancement may I hope from thee,
That no revenue hast but thy good spirits,   60
To feed and clothe thee? Why should the poor be
    flatter'd?
No, let the candied tongue lick absurd pomp,
And crook the pregnant hinges of the knee

64 **thrift:** profit.

71 **blood and judgment:** passion and reason.

81 **the very comment of thy soul:** all your powers of observation.
82 **occulted:** concealed.
83 **unkennel:** disclose.
84 **damned ghost:** demon, spirit of evil.
86 **Vulcan's stithy:** forge of Vulcan, god of fire.

89 **censure of his seeming:** judgment of his behavior.

91 **steal aught:** get away with anything.

93 **be idle:** seem unoccupied.

Where thrift may follow fawning. Dost thou hear?
Since my dear soul was mistress of her choice,   65
And could of men distinguish, her election
Hath seal'd thee for herself: for thou hast been
As one, in suff'ring all, that suffers nothing;
A man that fortune's buffets and rewards
Hast ta'en with equal thanks: and blest are those   70
Whose blood and judgment are so well commingled
That they are not a pipe for fortune's finger
To sound what stop she please. Give me that man
That is not passion's slave, and I will wear him
In my heart's core, aye, in my heart of heart,   75
As I do thee. Something too much of this.
There is a play tonight before the king;
One scene of it comes near the circumstance
Which I have told thee of my father's death:
I prithee, when thou seest that act afoot,   80
Even with the very comment of thy soul
Observe my uncle: if his occulted guilt
Do not itself unkennel in one speech
It is a damned ghost that we have seen,
And my imaginations arc as foul   85
As Vulcan's stithy. Give him heedful note;
For I mine eyes will rivet to his face,
And after we will both our judgments join
In censure of his seeming.
Horatio
                    Well, my lord: 90
If he steal aught the whilst this play is playing,
And 'scape detecting, I will pay the theft.
Hamlet
They are coming to the play: I must be idle:
Get you a place.

    Danish march. A flourish. Enter King, Queen, Polo-
    nius, Ophelia, Rosencrantz, Guildenstern, and other
    Lords attendant, with the Guard carrying torches.

96 **chameleon:** lizard believed to live on air.

106 **brute:** pun on Brutus and brute (or brutal).

King
How fares our cousin Hamlet?   95

Hamlet
Excellent, i' faith; of the chameleon's dish: I eat the
air, promise-crammed: you cannot feed capons so.

King
I have nothing with this answer, Hamlet; these words
are not mine.

Hamlet
No, nor mine now. [*To Polonius*] My lord, you   100
played once i' the university, you say?

Polonius
That did I, my lord, and was accounted a good actor.

Hamlet
What did you enact?

Polonius
I did enact Julius Cæsar: I was killed i' the Capitol;
Brutus killed me.   105

Hamlet
It was a brute part of him to kill so capital a calf
there. Be the players ready?

Rosencrantz
Aye, my lord; they stay upon your patience.

Queen
Come hither, my dear Hamlet, sit by me.

Hamlet
No, good mother, here's metal more attractive.   110

Polonius
[*To the King*]   O, ho! do you mark that?

Hamlet
Lady, shall I lie in your lap?
                    [*Lying down at Ophelia's feet.*

Ophelia
No, my lord.

133 suffer not thinking on: accept the fact he is forgotten.

134–135 hobby-horse is forgot: The Puritans had suppressed the old imitation horses once used in May Day celebrations.

Hamlet

I mean, my head upon your lap?

Ophelia

Aye, my lord.　　　　　　　　　　　　　　　　115

Hamlet

Do you think I meant country matters?

Ophelia

I think nothing, my lord.

Hamlet

That's a fair thought to lie between maids' legs.

Ophelia

What is, my lord?

Hamlet

Nothing.　　　　　　　　　　　　　　　　　120

Ophelia

You are merry, my lord.

Hamlet

Who, I?

Ophelia

Aye, my lord.

Hamlet

O God, your only jig-maker. What should a man do
but be merry? for, look you, how cheerfully my mother　125
looks, and my father died within 's two hours.

Ophelia

Nay, 'tis twice two months, my lord.

Hamlet

So long? Nay then, let the devil wear black, for I'll
have a suit of sables. O heavens! die two months
ago, and not forgotten yet? Then there's hope a great　130
man's memory may outlive his life half a year: but,
by 'r lady, he must build churches then; or else shall
he suffer not thinking on, with the hobby-horse,
whose epitaph is, "For, O, for, O, the hobby-horse
is forgot."　　　　　　　　　　　　　　　　　135

137 **miching mallecho:**   stealthy crime.

138 **argument:**   plot of a play.

145 **naught:**   naughty.

Hautboys play. The dumb-show enters.

Enter a King and a Queen very lovingly; the Queen embracing him and he her. She kneels, and makes show of protestation unto him. He takes her up, and declines his head upon her neck: lays him down upon a bank of flowers: she, seeing him asleep, leaves him. Anon comes in a fellow, takes off his crown, kisses it, and pours poison in the King's ears, and exit. The Queen returns; finds the King dead, and makes passionate action. The Poisoner, with some two or three Mutes, comes in again, seeming to lament with her. The dead body is carried away. The Poisoner woos the Queen with gifts: she seems loath and unwilling awhile, but in the end accepts his love.

[*Exeunt.*

Ophelia
What means this, my lord?

Hamlet
Marry, this is miching mallecho; it means mischief.

Ophelia
Belike this show imports the argument of the play.

Enter Prologue.

Hamlet
We shall know by this fellow: the players cannot keep counsel; they'll tell all.   140

Ophelia
Will he tell us what this show meant?

Hamlet
Aye, or any show that you'll show him: be not you ashamed to show, he'll not shame to tell you what it means.

Ophelia
You are naught, you are naught: I'll mark the play.   145

149 **posy:** motto.

152 **Phoebus' cart:** chariot of the sun god.
153 **Neptune's salt wash:** the oceans, Neptune being god of the sea.
Tellus' orbed ground: the earth, Tellus being goddess of the earth.
156 **Hymen:** god of marriage.

162 **distrust you:** am anxious about you.

164 **quantity:** proportion.

171 **operant:** active.
functions leave to do: cease operating.

Prologue

> For us, and for our tragedy,
> Here stooping to your clemency,
> We beg your hearing patiently.

Hamlet

> Is this a prologue, or the posy of a ring?

Ophelia

> 'Tis brief, my lord.   150

Hamlet

> As woman's love.

> *Enter two Players, King and Queen.*

Player King

> Full thirty times hath Phœbus' cart gone round
> Neptune's salt wash and Tellus' orbed ground,
> And thirty dozen moons with borrow'd sheen
> About the world have times twelve thirties been,   155
> Since love our hearts and Hymen did our hands
> Unite commutual in most sacred bands.

Player Queen

> So many journeys may the sun and moon
> Make us again count o'er ere love be done!
> But, woe is me, you are so sick of late,   160
> So far from cheer and from your former state,
> That I distrust you. Yet, though I distrust,
> Discomfort you, my lord, it nothing must:
> For women's fear and love holds quantity,
> In neither aught, or in extremity.   165
> Now, what my love is, proof hath made you know,
> And as my love is siz'd, my fear is so:
> Where love is great, the littlest doubts are fear,
> Where little fears grow great, great love grows there.

Player King

> Faith, I must leave thee, love, and shortly too;   170
> My operant powers their functions leave to do:
> And thou shalt live in this fair world behind,

179 **wormwood:**   a bitter plant.

180 **instances:**   motives.

187 **validity:**   strength.

189 **mellow:**   ripe.

195 **enactures:**   actions.

Honor'd, belov'd; and haply one as kind
For husband shalt thou—

Player Queen

O, confound the rest! 175
Such love must needs be treason in my breast:
In second husband let me be accurst!
None wed the second but who kill'd the first.

Hamlet
[*Aside*] Wormwood, wormwood.

Player Queen
The instances that second marriage move 180
Are base respects of thrift, but none of love:
A second time I kill my husband dead,
When second husband kisses me in bed.

Player King
I do believe you think what now you speak,
But what we do determine oft we break. 185
Purpose is but the slave to memory,
Of violent birth but poor validity:
Which now, like fruit unripe, sticks on the tree,
But fall unshaken when they mellow be.
Most necessary 'tis that we forget 190
To pay ourselves what to ourselves is debt:
What to ourselves in passion we propose,
The passion ending, doth the purpose lose.
The violence of either grief or joy
Their own enactures with themselves destroy: 195
Where joy most revels, grief doth most lament;
Grief joys, joy grieves, on slender accident.
This world is not for aye, nor 'tis not strange
That even our loves should with our fortunes change,
For 'tis a question left us yet to prove, 200
Whether love lead fortune or else fortune love.
The great man down, you mark his favorite flies;
The poor advanc'd makes friends of enemies:
And hitherto doth love on fortune tend;

207 **seasons:** matures.

217 **anchor's cheer:** hermit's fare.

224 **beguile:** while away.

For who not needs shall never lack a friend,   205
And who in want a hollow friend doth try
Directly seasons him his enemy.
But, orderly to end where I begun,
Our wills and fates do so contrary run,
That our devices still are overthrown,   210
Our thoughts are ours, their ends none of our own:
So think thou wilt no second husband wed,
But die thy thoughts when thy first lord is dead.

Player Queen
Nor earth to me give food nor heaven light!
Sport and repose lock from me day and night!   215
To desperation turn my trust and hope!
An anchor's cheer in prison be my scope!
Each opposite, that blanks the face of joy,
Meet what I would have well and it destroy!
Both here and hence pursue me lasting strife,   220
If, once a widow, ever I be wife!

Hamlet
If she should break it now!

Player King
'Tis deeply sworn. Sweet, leave me here awhile;
My spirits grow dull, and fain I would beguile
The tedious day with sleep.   225

                                        [*Sleeps.*

Player Queen
                              Sleep rock thy brain;
And never come mischance between us twain!

                                        [*Exit.*

Hamlet
Madam, how like you this play?

Queen
The lady doth protest too much, methinks.

Hamlet
O, but she'll keep her word.   230

231 **argument:** plot.

235 **Tropically:** figuratively.

240 **galled:** injured.
 jade: old horse.
 withers: high point of horse's back.

King

Have you heard the argument? Is there no offense in 't?

Hamlet

No, no, they do but jest, poison in jest; no offense i'
the world.

King

What do you call the play?

Hamlet

The Mouse-trap. Marry, how? Tropically. This play   235
is the image of a murder done in Vienna: Gonzago
is the duke's name; his wife, Baptista: you shall see
anon; 'tis a knavish piece of work; but what o' that?
your majesty, and we that have free souls, it touches
us not: let the galled jade wince, our withers are un-   240
wrung.

Enter Lucianus.

This is one Lucianus, nephew to the king.

Ophelia

You are as good as a chorus, my lord.

Hamlet

I could interpret between you and your love, if I
could see the puppets dallying.   245

Ophelia

You are keen, my lord, you are keen.

Hamlet

It would cost you a groaning to take off my edge.

Ophelia

Still better and worse.

Hamlet

So you must take your husbands. Begin, murderer;
pox, leave thy damnable faces, and begin. Come: the
croaking raven doth bellow for revenge.   250

Lucianus

Thoughts black, hands apt, drugs fit, and time agreeing;

255 **Hecate:** goddess of mischief and revenge.
  ban: curse.

265 **Give o'er:** stop.

269 **hart:** deer.
  ungalled: unhurt.

273 **turn Turk:** change completely for the worse.
274 **Provincial roses:** double-damask roses (like feathers, typical adornment on costumes worn by actors).
  razed: slashed.
275 **cry:** company.

Confederate season, else no creature seeing;
Thou mixture rank, of midnight weeds collected,
With Hecate's ban thrice blasted, thrice infected,   255
Thy natural magic and dire property,
On wholesome life usurp immediately.
           [Pours the poison into the sleeper's ear.

Hamlet
He poisons him i' the garden for his estate. His name's
Gonzago: the story is extant, and written in very choice
Italian: you shall see anon how the murderer gets the   260
love of Gonzago's wife.

Ophelia
The king rises.

Hamlet
What, frighted with false fire!

Queen
How fares my lord?

Polonius
Give o'er the play.   265

King
Give me some light. Away!

Polonius
Lights, lights, lights!
           [Exeunt all but Hamlet and Horatio.

Hamlet
   Why, let the stricken deer go weep,
       The hart ungalled play;
   For some must watch, while some must sleep: 270
       Thus runs the world away.

Would not this, sir, and a forest of feathers—if the
rest of my fortunes turn Turk with me—with two
Provincial roses on my razed shoes, get me a fellowship in a cry of players, sir?   275

Horatio
Half a share.

278 **Damon:** Damon and Pythias were close friends in legend.

280 **Jove:** another name for Jupiter, king of the gods (and a flattering reference to the elder Hamlet).

281 **pajock:** peacock (an unflattering reference to Claudius).

290 **perdy:** corruption of par Dieu, *by God*.

296 **distempered:** annoyed, disturbed.

Hamlet

A whole one, I.

> For thou dost know, O Damon dear,
> This realm dismantled was
> Of Jove himself; and now reigns here　　　280
> A very, very—pajock.

Horatio

You might have rhymed.

Hamlet

O good Horatio, I'll take the ghost's word for a thousand pound. Didst perceive?

Horatio

Very well, my lord.　　　　　　　　　　　285

Hamlet

Upon the talk of the poisoning?

Horatio

I did very well note him.

Hamlet

Ah, ha! Come, some music! come, the recorders!

> For if the king like not the comedy,
> Why then, belike, he likes it not, perdy.　　290

Come, some music!

Reenter Rosencrantz and Guildenstern.

Guildenstern

Good my lord, vouchsafe me a word with you.

Hamlet

Sir, a whole history.

Guildenstern

The king, sir—

Hamlet

Aye, sir, what of him?　　　　　　　　　295

Guildenstern

Is in his retirement marvelous distempered.

298 **choler:** rage.

300 **purgation:** cure.

Hamlet
　With drink, sir?

Guildenstern
　No, my lord, rather with choler.

Hamlet
　Your wisdom should show itself more richer to signify
　this to the doctor; for, for me to put him to his purga-　300
　tion would perhaps plunge him into far more choler.

Guildenstern
　Good my lord, put your discourse into some frame,
　and start not so wildly from my affair.

Hamlet
　I am tame, sir: pronounce.

Guildenstern
　The queen, your mother, in most great affliction of　305
　spirit, hath sent me to you.

Hamlet
　You are welcome.

Guildenstern
　Nay, good my lord, this courtesy is not of the right
　breed. If it shall please you to make me a wholesome
　answer, I will do your mother's commandment: if　310
　not, your pardon and my return shall be the end of
　my business.

Hamlet
　Sir, I cannot.

Guildenstern
　What, my lord?

Hamlet
　Make you a wholesome answer; my wit's diseased:　315
　but, sir, such answer as I can make, you shall com-
　mand; or rather, as you say, my mother: therefore
　no more, but to the matter: my mother, you say—

Rosencrantz
　Then thus she says; your behavior hath struck her

320 **admiration:**   wonder, astonishment.

324 **closet:**   room.

329 **pickers and stealers:**   hands.

338–339 **withdraw with you:**   have a word in private with you.
340 **toil:**   trap.

into amazement and admiration.   320

Hamlet

O wonderful son, that can so astonish a mother! But
is there no sequel at the heels of this mother's admiration? Impart.

Rosencrantz

She desires to speak with you in her closet, ere you go
to bed.   325

Hamlet

We shall obey, were she ten times our mother. Have
you any further trade with us?

Rosencrantz

My lord, you once did love me.

Hamlet

So I do still, by these pickers and stealers.

Rosencrantz

Good my lord, what is your cause of distemper? you   330
do surely bar the door upon your own liberty, if you
deny your griefs to your friend.

Hamlet

Sir, I lack advancement.

Rosencrantz

How can that be, when you have the voice of the
king himself for your succession in Denmark?   335

Hamlet

Aye, sir, but "while the grass grows"—the proverb is
something musty.

Reenter Players with recorders.

O, the recorders! let me see one. To withdraw with
you—why do you go about to recover the wind of me,
as if you would drive me into a toil?   340

Guildenstern

O, my lord, if my duty be too bold, my love is too
unmannerly.

350 **ventages:**   holes in the recorder.

364 **fret:**   irritate, annoy (with a pun on *fret,* part of a guitar).

Hamlet

I do not well understand that. Will you play upon
this pipe?

Guildenstern

My lord, I cannot.   345

Hamlet

I pray you.

Guildenstern

Believe me, I cannot.

Hamlet

I do beseech you.

Guildenstern

I know no touch of it, my lord.

Hamlet

It is as easy as lying: govern these ventages with your   350
fingers and thumb, give it breath with your mouth,
and it will discourse most eloquent music. Look you,
these are the stops.

Guildenstern

But these cannot I command to any utterance of har-
mony; I have not the skill.   355

Hamlet

Why, look you now, how unworthy a thing you make
of me! You would play upon me; you would seem to
know my stops; you would pluck out the heart of my
mystery; you would sound me from my lowest note
to the top of my compass: and there is much music,   360
excellent voice, in this little organ; yet cannot you
make it speak. 'Sblood, do you think I am easier to
be played on than a pipe? Call me what instrument
you will, though you can fret me, yet you cannot play
upon me.   365

Reenter Polonius.

God bless you, sir!

368 **presently:** immediately.

377 **to the top of my bent:** to the limit of my endurance.

386 **Nero:** Roman emperor, who murdered his mother.

Polonius
My lord, the queen would speak with you, and
presently.

Hamlet
Do you see yonder cloud that's almost in shape of a
camel?   370

Polonius
By the mass, and 'tis like a camel, indeed.

Hamlet
Methinks it is like a weasel.

Polonius
It is backed like a weasel.

Hamlet
Or like a whale?

Polonius
Very like a whale.   375

Hamlet
Then I will come to my mother by and by. They fool
me to the top of my bent. I will come by and by.

Polonius
I will say so.

                                        [*Exit Polonius.*

Hamlet
"By and by" is easily said. Leave me, friends.
                              [*Exeunt all but Hamlet.*
'Tis now the very witching time of night,   380
When churchyards yawn, and hell itself breathes out
Contagion to this world: now could I drink hot blood,
And do such bitter business as the day
Would quake to look on. Soft! now to my mother.
O heart, lose not thy nature; let not ever   385
The soul of Nero enter this firm bosom:
Let me be cruel, not unnatural:
I will speak daggers to her, but use none;
My tongue and soul in this be hypocrites;

390 **shent:** reproached.
391 **to give them seals:** to ratify by action.

5 **estate:** royal rank.

12 **peculiar:** private, personal.

14 **noyance:** injury, harm.
15 **weal:** well-being.

17 **gulf:** whirlpool.

21 **mortis'd:** cut to fit.
22 **annexment:** something connected.

How in my words soever she be shent,   390
To give them seals never, my soul, consent!

[*Exit.*

Scene 3. A room in the castle

Enter King, Rosencrantz, and Guildenstern.

King
    I like him not, nor stands it safe with us
    To let his madness range. Therefore prepare you;
    I your commission will forthwith dispatch,
    And he to England shall along with you:
    The terms of our estate may not endure   5
    Hazard so near us as doth hourly grow
    Out of his lunacies.
Guildenstern
                  We will ourselves provide:
    Most holy and religious fear it is
    To keep those many many bodies safe   10
    That live and feed upon your majesty.
Rosencrantz
    The single and peculiar life is bound
    With all the strength and armor of the mind
    To keep itself from noyance; but much more
    That spirit upon whose weal depends and rests   15
    The lives of many. The cease of majesty
    Dies not alone, but like a gulf doth draw
    What's near it with it; it is a massy wheel,
    Fix'd on the summit of the highest mount,
    To whose huge spokes ten thousand lesser things   20
    Are mortis'd and adjoin'd; which, when it falls,
    Each small annexment, petty consequence,

30 **arras:** tapestry.
31 **warrant:** guarantee.
   tax him home: scold him thoroughly.
33 **meet:** fitting.

35 **of vantage:** from a good place of concealment.

40 **primal eldest curse:** the first murder, in the Bible: the slaying of Abel by his brother Cain.

Attends the boist'rous ruin. Never alone
Did the king sigh, but with a general groan.

King

Arm you, I pray you, to this speedy voyage,　　　　25
For we will fetters put about this fear,
Which now goes too free-footed.

Rosencrantz and Guildenstern

We will haste us.

[*Exeunt Rosencrantz and Guildenstern.*

Enter Polonius.

Polonius

My lord, he's going to his mother's closet:
Behind the arras I'll convey myself,　　　　30
To hear the process: I'll warrant she'll tax him home:
And, as you said, and wisely was it said,
'Tis meet that some more audience than a mother,
Since nature makes them partial, should o'erhear
The speech, of vantage. Fare you well, my liege:　　　　35
I'll call upon you ere you go to bed,
And tell you what I know.

King

Thanks, dear my lord.

[*Exit Polonius.*

O, my offense is rank, it smells to heaven;
It hath the primal eldest curse upon 't,　　　　40
A brother's murder. Pray can I not,
Though inclination be as sharp as will:
My stronger guilt defeats my strong intent,
And like a man to double business bound,
I stand in pause where I shall first begin,　　　　45
And both neglect. What if this cursed hand
Were thicker than itself with brother's blood,
Is there not rain enough in the sweet heavens
To wash it white as snow? Whereto serves mercy
But to confront the visage of offense?　　　　50

63 **buys out:** bribes.

71 **limed:** caught, as with birdlime (a sticky substance for catching small birds).
72 **make assay:** try.

78 **scann'd:** carefully considered.

83 **full of bread:** filled with earthly imperfections.

And what's in prayer but this twofold force,
To be forestalled ere we come to fall,
Or pardon'd being down? Then I'll look up;
My fault is past. But O, what form of prayer
Can serve my turn? "Forgive me my foul murder?"　　55
That cannot be, since I am still possess'd
Of those effects for which I did the murder,
My crown, mine own ambition and my queen.
May one be pardon'd and retain th' offense?
In the corrupted currents of this world　　　　60
Offense's gilded hand may shove by justice,
And oft 'tis seen the wicked prize itself
Buys out the law: but 'tis not so above;
There is no shuffling, there the action lies
In his true nature, and we ourselves compell'd　　65
Even to the teeth and forehead of our faults
To give in evidence. What then? what rests?
Try what repentance can: what can it not?
Yet what can it when one can not repent?
O wretched state! O bosom black as death;　　70
O limed soul, that struggling to be free
Art more engag'd! Help, angels! make assay!
Bow, stubborn knees, and, heart with strings of steel,
Be soft as sinews of the new-born babe!
All may be well.　　　　75

　　　　　　　　　　[*Retires and kneels.*

　　Enter Hamlet.

Hamlet
Now might I do it pat, now he is praying;
And now I'll do 't: and so he goes to heaven:
And so am I reveng'd. That would be scann'd;
A villain kills my father; and for that,
I, his sole son, do this same villain send　　　80
To heaven.
O, this is hire and salary, not revenge.
He took my father grossly, full of bread,

91 **hent:** hold, seizure.

98 **stays:** awaits me.
99 **physic:** medicine.

1 **lay home:** speak bluntly.

4 **heat:** anger.
sconce me: place myself.
5 **round:** direct.

With all his crimes broad blown, as flush as May;
And how his audit stands who knows save heaven?   85
But in our circumstance and course of thought,
'Tis heavy with him: and am I then reveng'd,
To take him in the purging of his soul,
When he is fit and season'd for his passage?
No.   90
Up, sword, and know thou a more horrid hent:
When he is drunk asleep, or in his rage,
Or in th' incestuous pleasure of his bed;
At game, a-swearing, or about some act
That has no relish of salvation in 't;   95
Then trip him, that his heels may kick at heaven
And that his soul may be as damn'd and black
As hell, whereto it goes. My mother stays:
This physic but prolongs thy sickly days.

                            [*Exit.*

King
[*Rising*] My words fly up, my thoughts remain below: 100
Words without thoughts never to heaven go.

                            [*Exit.*

Scene 4. The Queen's closet

Enter Queen and Polonius.

Polonius
He will come straight. Look you lay home to him:
Tell him his pranks have been too broad to bear with,
And that your grace hath screen'd and stood between
Much heat and him. I'll sconce me even here.
Pray you, be round with him.   5
Hamlet
            [*Within*]   Mother, mother, mother!

17 **rood:** cross.

22 **glass:** mirror.

Queen
  I'll warrant you; fear me not. Withdraw, I hear him
  coming.

  [*Polonius hides behind the arras.*

  Enter Hamlet.

Hamlet
  Now, mother, what's the matter?

Queen
  Hamlet, thou hast thy father much offended.   10

Hamlet
  Mother, you have my father much offended.

Queen
  Come, come, you answer with an idle tongue.

Hamlet
  Go, go, you question with a wicked tongue.

Queen
  Why, how now, Hamlet!

Hamlet
                            What's the matter now?   15

Queen
  Have you forget me?

Hamlet
                          No, by the rood, not so:
  You are the queen, your husband's brother's wife;
  And—would it were not so!—you are my mother.

Queen
  Nay, then, I'll set those to you that can speak.   20

Hamlet
  Come, come, and sit you down; you shall not budge;
  You go not till I set you up a glass
  Where you may see the inmost part of you.

Queen
  What wilt thou do? thou wilt not murder me?
  Help, help, ho!   25

43 **brass'd:** hardened.

Polonius
  [Behind]   What, ho! help, help, help!

Hamlet
  [Drawing]   How now! a rat? Dead, for a ducat,
      dead!

                    [Makes a pass through the arras.

Polonius
  [Behind]   O, I am slain!

                              [Falls and dies.

Queen
                    O me, what hast thou done?   30

Hamlet
  Nay, I know not: is it the king?

Queen
  Oh, what a rash and bloody deed is this!

Hamlet
  A bloody deed! almost as bad, good mother,
  As kill a king, and marry with his brother.

Queen
  As kill a king!   35

Hamlet
                    Aye, lady, 'twas my word.
          [Lifts up the arras and discovers Polonius.
  Thou wretched, rash, intruding fool, farewell!
  I took thee for thy better: take thy fortune;
  Thou find'st to be too busy is some danger.
  Leave wringing of your hands: peace! sit you down,   40
  And let me wring your heart: for so I shall,
  If it be made of penetrable stuff;
  If damned custom have not brass'd it so,
  That it be proof and bulwark against sense.

Queen
  What have I done, that thou darest wag thy tongue   45
  In noise so rude against me?

53 **contraction:**   making of the marriage contract.

55 **rhapsody:**   meaningless jumble.
56 **mass:**   the earth.
57 **tristful visage:**   sad face.
   as against the doom: as at the approach of Judgment Day.

60 **index:**   prologue, preface.

62 **counterfeit presentment:**   portrait.

64 **Hyperion:**   god of the sun, symbol of beauty.
   Jove: Jupiter, king of the gods.
65 **Mars:**   god of war.
66 **Mercury:**   messenger of the gods.

74 **leave to feed:**   stop feeding.
75 **batten:**   grow fat.

79 **Sense:**   feeling, sensibility.

Hamlet

                  Such an act
That blurs the grace and blush of modesty,
Calls virtue hypocrite, takes off the rose
From the fair forehead of an innocent love,   50
And sets a blister there; makes marriage vows
As false as dicers' oaths: O, such a deed
As from the body of contraction plucks
The very soul, and sweet religion makes
A rhapsody of words: heaven's face doth glow;   55
Yea, this solidity and compound mass,
With tristful visage, as against the doom,
Is thought-sick at the act.

Queen

                   Aye me, what act,
That roars so loud and thunders in the index?   60

Hamlet

Look here, upon this picture, and on this,
The counterfeit presentment of two brothers.
See what a grace was seated on this brow;
Hyperion's curls, the front of Jove himself,
An eye like Mars, to threaten and command;   65
A station like the herald Mercury
New-lighted on a heaven-kissing hill;
A combination and a form indeed,
Where every god did seem to set his seal
To give the world assurance of a man: 70
This was your husband. Look you now, what follows:
Here is your husband; like a mildew'd ear,
Blasting his wholesome brother. Have you eyes?
Could you on this fair mountain leave to feed,
And batten on this moor? Ha! have you eyes?   75
You cannot call it love, for at your age
The hey-day in the blood is tame, it's humble,
And waits upon the judgment: and what judgment
Would step from this to this? Sense sure you have,

82 **thrall'd:** enslaved.

85 **cozen'd:** cheated.
   hoodman-blind: blind-man's bluff.
87 **sans:** without.

89 **mope:** act so foolishly.

91 **mutine:** mutiny.

96 **reason panders will:** reason indulges will, rather than re-
   strains it.

100 **tinct:** dye, color.

102 **enseamed:** defiled, filthy.

109 **tithe:** tenth.
110 **precedent:** former.
111 **cutpurse:** thief.

Else could you not have motion: but sure that sense   80
Is apoplex'd: for madness would not err,
Nor sense to ecstasy was ne'er so thrall'd
But it reserv'd some quantity of choice,
To serve in such a difference. What devil was 't
That thus hath cozen'd you at hoodman-blind?   85
Eyes without feeling, feeling without sight,
Ears without hands or eyes, smelling sans all,
Or but a sickly part of one true sense
Could not so mope.
O shame! where is thy blush? Rebellious hell,   90
If thou canst mutine in a matron's bones,
To flaming youth let virtue be as wax
And melt in her own fire: proclaim no shame
When the compulsive ardor gives the charge,
Since frost itself as actively doth burn,   95
And reason panders will.

Queen

                   O Hamlet, speak no more:
Thou turn'st mine eyes into my very soul,
And there I see such black and grained spots
As will not leave their tinct.   100

Hamlet

                   Nay, but to live
In the rank sweat of an enseamed bed,
Stew'd in corruption, honeying and making love
Over the nasty sty—

Queen

                   O, speak to me no more;   105
These words like daggers enter in my ears;
No more, sweet Hamlet!

Hamlet

                   A murderer and a villain;
A slave that is not twentieth part the tithe
Of your precedent lord; a vice of kings;   110
A cutpurse of the empire and the rule,

127 **conceit:** imagination.

132 **incorporal:** insubstantial.

135 **excrements:** outgrowths.

That from a shelf the precious diadem stole
And put it in his pocket!

Queen

                    No more!

Hamlet

A king of shreds and patches—   115

Enter Ghost.

Save me, and hover o'er me with your wings,
You heavenly guards! What would your gracious
    figure?

Queen

Alas, he's mad!

Hamlet

Do you not come your tardy son to chide,
That, laps'd in time and passion, lets go by   120
Th' important acting of your dread command?
O, say!

Ghost

Do not forget: this visitation
Is but to whet thy almost blunted purpose.
But look, amazement on thy mother sits: 125
O, step between her and her fighting soul:
Conceit in weakest bodies strongest works:
Speak to her, Hamlet.

Hamlet

                    How is it with you, lady?

Queen

Alas, how is 't with you,   130
That you do bend your eye on vacancy
And with th' incorporal air do hold discourse?
Forth at your eyes your spirits wildly peep;
And, as the sleeping soldiers in th' alarm,
Your bedded hairs, like life in excrements,   135
Stand up and stand an end. O gentle son,

141 **capable:** capable of feeling, susceptible.

151 **habit:** clothes.

154 **ecstasy:** madness.

Upon the heat and flame of thy distemper
Sprinkle cool patience. Whereon do you look?
Hamlet
On him, on him! Look you how pale he glares!
His form and cause conjoin'd, preaching to stones,   140
Would make them capable. Do not look upon me,
Lest with this piteous action you convert
My stern effects: then what I have to do
Will want true color; tears perchance for blood.
Queen
To whom do you speak this?   145
Hamlet
                              Do you see nothing there?
Queen
Nothing at all; yet all that is I see.
Hamlet
Nor did you nothing hear?
Queen
                              No, nothing but ourselves.
Hamlet
Why, look you there! look, how it steals away!   150
My father, in his habit as he liv'd!
Look, where he goes, even now, out at the portal!
                              [*Exit Ghost.*
Queen
This is the very coinage of your brain:
This bodiless creation ecstasy
Is very cunning in.   155
Hamlet
                              Ecstasy!
My pulse, as yours, doth temperately keep time,
And makes as healthful music: it is not madness
That I have utter'd: bring me to the test,
And I the matter will reword, which madness   160
Would gambol from. Mother, for love of grace,

162 **flattering unction:** soothing ointment.

170 **fatness:** grossness.
    pursy: fat with pampering.
172 **curb:** cringe.

Lay not that flattering unction to your soul,
That not your trespass but my madness speaks:
It will but skin and film the ulcerous place,
Whiles rank corruption, mining all within,   165
Infects unseen. Confess yourself to heaven;
Repent what's past, avoid what is to come,
And do not spread the compost on the weeds,
To make them ranker. Forgive me this my virtue,
For in the fatness of these pursy times   170
Virtue itself of vice must pardon beg,
Yea, curb and woo for leave to do him good.

Queen
O Hamlet, thou hast cleft my heart in twain.

Hamlet
O, throw away the worser part of it,
And live the purer with the other half.   175
Good night: but go not to my uncle's bed;
Assume a virtue, if you have it not.
That monster, custom, who all sense doth eat,
Of habits devil, is angel yet in this,
That to the use of actions fair and good   180
He likewise gives a frock or livery,
That aptly is put on. Refrain tonight,
And that shall lend a kind of easiness
To the next abstinence; the next more easy;
For use almost can change the stamp of nature,   185
And either curb the devil, or throw him out
With wondrous potency. Once more, good night:
And when you are desirous to be blest,
I'll blessing beg of you. For this same lord,
                              [*Pointing to Polonius.*
I do repent: but heaven hath pleas'd it so,   190
To punish me with this, and this with me,
That I must be their scourge and minister.
I will bestow him, and will answer well
The death I gave him. So, again, good night.

200 **bloat:** bloated.

202 **reechy:** reeking, foul.

208 **paddock:** toad.
   gib: tomcat.

212 **like the famous ape:** reference to a lost fable, apparently about an ape that died trying to imitate the birds.

213 **try conclusions:** make experiments.

I must be cruel, only to be kind: 195
Thus bad begins, and worse remains behind.
One word more, good lady.

Queen

What shall I do?

Hamlet

Not this, by no means, that I bid you do:
Let the bloat king tempt you again to bed;   200
Pinch wanton on your cheek, call you his mouse;
And let him, for a pair of reechy kisses,
Or paddling in your neck with his damn'd fingers,
Make you to ravel all this matter out,
That I essentially am not in madness,   205
But mad in craft. 'Twere good you let him know;
For who, that's but a queen, fair, sober, wise,
Would from a paddock, from a bat, a gib,
Such dear concernings hide? who would do so?
No, in despite of sense and secrecy,   210
Unpeg the basket on the house's top,
Let the birds fly, and like the famous ape,
To try conclusions, in the basket creep
And break your own neck down.

Queen

Be thou assur'd, if words be made of breath   215
And breath of life, I have no life to breathe
What thou hast said to me.

Hamlet

I must to England; you know that?

Queen

Alack,
I had forgot: 'tis so concluded on.   220

Hamlet

There's letters seal'd: and my two schoolfellows,
Whom I will trust as I will adders fang'd,
They bear the mandate; they must sweep my way,

225 **enginer:** engineer.
226 **Hoist with his own petar:** blown up by his own bomb.

4 **Bestow this place on us:** leave us alone.

And marshal me to knavery. Let it work;
For 'tis the sport to have the enginer   225
Hoist with his own petar: and 't shall go hard
But I will delve one yard below their mines,
And blow them at the moon: O, 'tis most sweet
When in one line two crafts directly meet.
This man shall set me packing: 230
I'll lug the guts into the neighbor room.
Mother, good night. Indeed this counselor
Is now most still, most secret and most grave,
Who was in life a foolish prating knave.
Come, sir, to draw toward an end with you.   235
Good night, mother.

    [*Exeunt severally; Hamlet dragging in Polonius.*

ACT IV

Scene 1. *A room in the castle*

Enter King, Queen, Rosencrantz, and Guildenstern.

King

There's matter in these sighs, these profound heaves:
You must translate: 'tis fit we understand them.
Where is your son?

Queen

Bestow this place on us a little while.

        [*Exeunt Rosencrantz and Guildenstern.*
Ah, mine own lord, what have I seen tonight!   5

King

What, Gertrude? How does Hamlet?

11 **brainish apprehension:**   brainsick delusion.

18 **providence:**   foresight.
19 **out of haunt:**   in seclusion.

25 **draw apart:**   take away.

27 **mineral:**   mine.

33 **countenance:**   face up to.

Queen

  Mad as the sea and wind, when both contend
  Which is the mightier: in his lawless fit,
  Behind the arras hearing something stir,
  Whips out his rapier, cries "A rat, a rat!"   10
  And in this brainish apprehension kills
  The unseen good old man.

King

                    O heavy deed!
  It had been so with us, had we been there:
  His liberty is full of threats to all,   15
  To you yourself, to us, to every one.
  Alas, how shall this bloody deed be answer'd?
  It will be laid to us, whose providence
  Should have kept short, restrain'd and out of haunt,
  This mad young man: but so much was our love,   20
  We would not understand what was most fit,
  But, like the owner of a foul disease,
  To keep it from divulging, let it feed
  Even on the pith of life. Where is he gone?

Queen

  To draw apart the body he hath kill'd: 25
  O'er whom his very madness, like some ore
  Among a mineral of metals base,
  Shows itself pure; he weeps for what is done.

King

  O Gertrude, come away!
  The sun no sooner shall the mountains touch,   30
  But we will ship him hence: and this vile deed
  We must, with all our majesty and skill,
  Both countenance and excuse. Ho, Guildenstern!

Reenter Rosencrantz and Guildenstern.

  Friends both, go join you with some further aid:
  Hamlet in madness hath Polonius slain,   35
  And from his mother's closet hath he dragg'd him:

43 **blank:**   the white mark in a target.

45 **woundless:**   invulnerable.

Go seek him out; speak fair, and bring the body
Into the chapel. I pray you, haste in this.
[Exeunt Rosencrantz and Guildenstern.
Come, Gertrude, we'll call up our wisest friends;
And let them know both what we mean to do,   40
And what's untimely done; [so haply slander,]
Whose whisper o'er the world's diameter
As level as the cannon to his blank
Transports his poison'd shot, may miss our name
And hit the woundless air. O, come away!   45
My soul is full of discord and dismay.

[Exeunt.

Scene 2. *Another room in the castle*

Enter Hamlet.

Hamlet
    Safely stow'd.
Rosencrantz and Guildenstern
    [*Within*]   Hamlet! Lord Hamlet.
Hamlet
    But soft, what noise? who calls on Hamlet?
    O, here they come.

    Enter Rosencrantz and Guildenstern.

Rosencrantz
    What have you done, my lord, with the dead body?   5
Hamlet
    Compounded it with dust, whereto 'tis kin.
Rosencrantz
    Tell us where 'tis, that we may take it thence
    And bear it to the chapel.

12 **replication:** reply, answer.

15 **countenance:** favor.

29 **Hide fox, and all after:** a phrase from a game similar to hide-and-seek.

Hamlet
Do not believe it.

Rosencrantz
Believe what?   10

Hamlet
That I can keep your counsel and not mine own.
Besides, to be demanded of a sponge! what replication
should be made by the son of a king?

Rosencrantz
Take you me for a sponge, my lord?

Hamlet
Aye, sir; that soaks up the king's countenance, his re-   15
wards, his authorities. But such officers do the king
best service in the end: he keeps them, like an ape,
in the corner of his jaw; first mouthed, to be last swallowed: when he needs what you have gleaned, it is but
squeezing you, and, sponge, you shall be dry again.   20

Rosencrantz
I understand you not, my lord.

Hamlet
I am glad of it: a knavish speech sleeps in a foolish
ear.

Rosencrantz
My lord, you must tell us where the body is, and go
with us to the king.   25

Hamlet
The body is with the king, but the king is not with
the body. The king is a thing—

Guildenstern
A thing, my lord?

Hamlet
Of nothing: bring me to him. Hide fox, and all after.

[*Exeunt.*

4 **distracted multitude:** confused common people.

6 **scourge:** punishment.

9 **deliberate pause:** well-planned delay.
10 **appliance:** remedy.

Scene 3. *Another room in the castle*

Enter King, attended.

King
I have sent to seek him, and to find the body.
How dangerous is it that this man goes loose!
Yet must not we put the strong law on him:
He's lov'd of the distracted multitude,
Who like not in their judgment, but their eyes;   5
And where 'tis so, the offender's scourge is weigh'd,
But never the offense. To bear all smooth and even,
This sudden sending away must seem
Deliberate pause: diseases desperate grown
By desperate appliance are relieved,   10
Or not at all.

Enter Rosencrantz.

How now! what hath befall'n?

Rosencrantz
Where the dead body is bestow'd, my lord,
We cannot get from him.

King
But where is he?   15

Rosencrantz
Without, my lord; guarded, to know your pleasure.

King
Bring him before us.

Rosencrantz
Ho, Guildenstern! bring in my lord.

Enter Hamlet and Guildenstern.

King
Now, Hamlet, where's Polonius?

23 **convocation:**   meeting.

33 **progress:**   journey made by a ruler in his own country.

Hamlet
  At supper.   20
King
  At supper! where?
Hamlet
  Not where he eats, but where he is eaten: a certain
  convocation of public worms are e'en at him. Your
  worm is your only emperor for diet: we fat all crea-
  tures else to fat us, and we fat ourselves for maggots: 25
  your fat king and your lean beggar is but variable ser-
  vice, two dishes, but to one table: that's the end.
King
  Alas, alas!
Hamlet
  A man may fish with the worm that hath eat of a
  king, and eat of the fish that hath fed of that worm.   30
King
  What dost thou mean by this?
Hamlet
  Nothing but to show you how a king may go a
  progress through the guts of a beggar.
King
  Where is Polonius?
Hamlet
  In heaven; send thither to see: if your messenger find   35
  him not there, seek him i' the other place yourself.
  But indeed, if you find him not within this month,
  you shall nose him as you go up the stairs into the
  lobby.
King
  [*To Attendants.*]   Go seek him there.   40
Hamlet
  He will stay till you come.
                              [*Exeunt Attendants.*

43 **tender:** have a care for.

47 **tend:** wait.

64 **sense:** awareness of my power.
65 **cicatrice:** scar.

King

    Hamlet, this deed, for thine especial safety,
    Which we do tender, as we dearly grieve
    For that which thou hast done, must send thee hence
    With fiery quickness: therefore prepare thyself;   45
    The bark is ready and the wind at help,
    Th' associates tend, and every thing is bent
    For England.

Hamlet

            For England?

King

                  Aye, Hamlet.   50

Hamlet

                           Good.

King

    So is it, if thou knew'st our purposes.

Hamlet

    I see a cherub that sees them. But, come; for En-
    gland! Farewell, dear mother.

King

    Thy loving father, Hamlet.   55

Hamlet

    My mother: father and mother is man and wife;
    man and wife is one flesh, and so, my mother. Come,
    for England!

                                 [*Exit.*

King

    Follow him at foot; tempt him with speed abroad;
    Delay it not; I'll have him hence tonight: 60
    Away! for every thing is seal'd and done
    That else leans on th' affair: pray you, make haste.
          [*Exeunt Rosencrantz and Guildenstern.*
    And, England, if my love thou hold'st at aught—
    As my great power thereof may give thee sense,
    Since yet thy cicatrice looks raw and red   65
    After the Danish sword, and thy free awe

67 **set:** regard, esteem.
68 **process:** decree.
69 **congruing:** agreeing.
70 **present:** immediate.
71 **hectic:** continuing fever.

73 **haps:** fortune.

3 **conveyance:** escort.

9 **softly:** slowly.

Pays homage to us—thou mayst not coldly set
Our sovereign process; which imports at full,
By letters congruing to that effect,
The present death of Hamlet. Do it, England;　　70
For like the hectic in my blood he rages,
And thou must cure me; till I know 'tis done,
Howe'er my haps, my joys were ne'er begun.

　　　　　　　　　　　　　　　　　[*Exit.*

Scene 4. A plain in Denmark

Enter Fortinbras, a Captain, and Soldiers, marching.

Fortinbras
　Go, captain, from me greet the Danish king;
　Tell him that by his license Fortinbras
　Craves the conveyance of a promis'd march
　Over his kingdom. You know the rendezvous.
　If that his majesty would aught with us,　　5
　We shall express our duty in his eye;
　And let him know so.
Captain
　　　　　　I will do 't, my lord.
Fortinbras
　Go softly on.

　　　　　　[*Exeunt Fortinbras and Soldiers.*

　Enter Hamlet, Rosencrantz, Guildenstern, and
　others.

Hamlet
　Good sir, whose powers are these?　　10
Captain
　They are of Norway, sir.

16 **main:** country as a whole.

18 **addition:** unnecessary detail.

21 **farm:** lease.

23 **ranker:** richer, greater.
fee: fee simple, outright.

28 **imposthume:** abscess, hidden infection, cancer.

Hamlet
How purpos'd, sir, I pray you?

Captain
Against some part of Poland.

Hamlet
Who commands them, sir?

Captain
The nephew to old Norway, Fortinbras.   15

Hamlet
Goes it against the main of Poland, sir,
Or for some frontier?

Captain
Truly to speak, and with no addition,
We go to gain a little patch of ground
That hath in it no profit but the name.   20
To pay five ducats, five, I would not farm it;
Nor will it yield to Norway or the Pole
A ranker rate, should it be sold in fee.

Hamlet
Why, then the Polack never will defend it.

Captain
Yes, it is already garrison'd.   25

Hamlet
Two thousand souls and twenty thousand ducats
Will not debate the question of this straw:
This is th' imposthume of much wealth and peace,
That inward breaks, and shows no cause without
Why the man dies. I humbly thank you, sir.   30

Captain
God be wi' you, sir.

[*Exit.*

Rosencrantz
                    Will 't please you go, my lord?

Hamlet
I'll be with you straight. Go a little before.

38 **discourse:** reason, intelligence.

41 **fust:** become moldy.

43 **event:** result.

56 **argument:** subject in dispute.

65 **Whereon the numbers cannot try the cause:** not large enough to hold the number of men fighting there.

[Exeunt all but Hamlet

How all occasions do inform against me,
And spur my dull revenge! What is a man,   35
If his chief good and market of his time
Be but to sleep and feed? a beast, no more.
Sure, he that made us with such large discourse,
Looking before and after, gave us not
That capability and god-like reason   40
To fust in us unus'd. Now, whether it be
Bestial oblivion, or some craven scruple
Of thinking too precisely on th' event—
A thought which, quarter'd, hath but one part wisdom
And ever three parts coward—I do not know   45
Why yet I live to say "this thing's to do,"
Sith I have cause, and will, and strength, and means,
To do 't. Examples gross as earth exhort me:
Witness this army, of such mass and charge,
Led by a delicate and tender prince,   50
Whose spirit with divine ambition puff'd
Makes mouths at the invisible event,
Exposing what is mortal and unsure
To all that fortune, death and danger dare,
Even for an eggshell. Rightly to be great   55
Is not to stir without great argument,
But greatly to find quarrel in a straw
When honor's at the stake. How stand I then,
That have a father kill'd, a mother stain'd,
Excitements of my reason and my blood,   60
And let all sleep, while to my shame I see
The imminent death of twenty thousand men,
That for a fantasy and trick of frame
Go to their graves like beds, fight for a plot
Whereon the numbers cannot try the cause,   65
Which is not tomb enough and continent
To hide the slain? O, from this time forth,
My thoughts be bloody, or be nothing worth!

[Exit.

2 **distract:** distracted, disturbed.

7 **spurns enviously:** kicks angrily.

10 **collection:** attempt to gather meaning.
   aim: guess.

13 **thought:** meaning.

19 **toy:** trifle.
   amiss: misfortune.
20 **artless jealousy:** unfounded suspicion.

Scene 5. Elsinore. A room in the castle

Enter Queen, Horatio, and a Gentleman.

Queen
I will not speak with her.
Gentleman
She is importunate, indeed distract:
Her mood will needs be pitied.
Queen
                          What would she have?
Gentleman
She speaks much of her father, says she hears   5
There's tricks i' the world, and hems and beats her
     heart,
Spurns enviously at straws; speaks things in doubt,
That carry but half sense: her speech is nothing,
Yet the unshaped use of it doth move
The hearers to collection; they aim at it,   10
And botch the words up fit to their own thoughts;
Which, as her winks and nods and gestures yield them,
Indeed would make one think there might be thought,
Though nothing sure, yet much unhappily.
Horatio
'Twere good she were spoken with, for she may strew   15
Dangerous conjectures in ill-breeding minds.
Queen
Let her come in.
                     [*Exit Gentleman.*
[*Aside*]   To my sick soul, as sin's true nature is,
Each toy seems prologue to some great amiss:
So full of artless jealousy is guilt,   20
It spills itself in fearing to be spilt.

Reenter Gentleman, with Ophelia.

26 **cockle hat:**   hat with a scallop shell (the badge of pilgrims).
27 **shoon:**   shoes.

39 **Larded:**   garnished.

43 **'ild:**   reward.

Ophelia
  Where is the beauteous majesty of Denmark?
Queen
  How now, Ophelia!
Ophelia
  [*Sings*]   How should I your true love know
              From another one?   25
              By his cockle hat and staff
              And his sandal shoon.
Queen
  Alas, sweet lady, what imports this song?
Ophelia
  Say you? nay, pray you, mark.
  [*Sings*]   He is dead and gone, lady,   30
              He is dead and gone;
              At his head a grass-green turf,
              At his heels a stone.
  Oh, oh!
Queen
                    Nay, but Ophelia—   35
Ophelia
                            Pray you, mark.
  [*Sings*]   White his shroud as the mountain snow—

      Enter King.

Queen
  Alas, look here, my lord.
Ophelia
  [*Sings*]   Larded with sweet flowers;
              Which bewept to the grave did go   40
              With true-love showers.
King
  How do you, pretty lady?
Ophelia
  Well, God 'ild you! They say the owl was a baker's

43–44 **the owl was a baker's daughter:** reference to a legend in which a baker's daughter was changed into an owl because she was reluctant to give bread to Christ.

46 **conceit upon:** obsession with.

49 **Saint Valentine:** the patron saint of lovers.
50 **betime:** early.

54 **dupp'd:** opened.

59 **Gis:** Jesus.

daughter. Lord, we know what we are, but know not
what we may be. God be at your table!   45

King

Conceit upon her father.

Ophelia

Pray you, let's have no words of this; but when they
ask you what it means, say you this:

[*Sings*]   Tomorrow is Saint Valentine's day
                  All in the morning betime,   50
              And I a maid at your window,
                  To be your Valentine.
              Then up he rose, and donn'd his clothes,
                  And dupp'd the chamber-door;
              Let in the maid, that out a maid   55
                  Never departed more.

King

Pretty Ophelia!

Ophelia

Indeed, la, without an oath, I'll make an end on 't:

[*Sings*]   By Gis and by Saint Charity,
                  Alack, and fie for shame!   60
              Young men will do 't, if they come to 't;
                  By cock, they are to blame.
              Quoth she, before you tumbled me,
                  You promised me to wed.

He answers: 65

              So would I ha' done, by yonder sun,
                  An thou hadst not come to my bed.

King

How long hath she been thus?

Ophelia

I hope all will be well. We must be patient: but I
cannot choose but weep, to think they should lay him   70
i' the cold ground. My brother shall know of it: and
so I thank you for your good counsel. Come, my

81 **remove:** removal, banishment.
muddied: stirred up.
83 **greenly:** foolishly.

84 **In hugger-mugger:** in secrecy and in haste.
inter: bury.
86 **pictures:** appearances.

89 **clouds:** clouds of uncertainty.
90 **buzzers:** whisperers.

92 **of matter beggar'd:** without fact or substance.
93 **arraign:** accuse.

95 **murdering-piece:** kind of cannon firing a scattering charge.
96 **superfluous death:** suffering many wounds, more than enough to kill.

98 **Switzers:** Swiss guards.

coach! Good night, ladies; good night, sweet ladies;
good night, good night.

[*Exit.*

King
Follow her close; give her good watch, I pray you.   75
[*Exit Horatio.*
O, this is the poison of deep grief; it springs
All from her father's death. O Gertrude, Gertrude,
When sorrows come, they come not single spies,
But in battalions! First, her father slain:
Next, your son gone; and he most violent author   80
Of his own just remove: the people muddied,
Thick and unwholesome in their thoughts and whispers,
For good Polonius' death; and we have done but
          greenly,
In hugger-mugger to inter him: poor Ophelia
Divided from herself and her fair judgment,   85
Without the which we are pictures, or mere beasts:
Last, and as much containing as all these,
Her brother is in secret come from France,
Feeds on his wonder, keeps himself in clouds,
And wants not buzzers to infect his ear   90
With pestilent speeches of his father's death;
Wherein necessity, of matter beggar'd,
Will nothing stick our person to arraign
In ear and ear. O my dear Gertrude, this,
Like to a murdering-piece, in many places   95
Gives me superfluous death.

[*A noise within.*

Queen
                    Alack, what noise is this?

King
Where are my Switzers? Let them guard the door.

Enter another Gentleman.

What is the matter?

101 **overpeering:** overflowing.

     list: boundary.

103 **head:** armed force.

105 **as the world were now but to begin:** as though there were no helpful precedents.

112 **counter:** wrong direction (as hounds will sometimes follow the wrong scent).

Gentleman

     Save yourself, my lord: 100
The ocean, overpeering of his list,
Eats not the flats with more impetuous haste
Than young Laertes, in a riotous head,
O'erbears your officers. The rabble call him lord;
And, as the world were now but to begin,   105
Antiquity forgot, custom not known,
The ratifiers and props of every word,
They cry "Choose we; Laertes shall be king!"
Caps, hands and tongues applaud it to the clouds,
"Laertes shall be king, Laertes king!"   110

Queen
How cheerfully on the false trail they cry!
O, this is counter, you false Danish dogs!
           [Noise within.

King
The doors are broke.

  Enter Laertes, armed; Danes following.

Laertes
Where is this king? Sirs, stand you all without.

Danes
No, let's come in.   115

Laertes
     I pray you, give me leave.

Danes
We will, we will.
     [They retire without the door.

Laertes
I thank you: keep the door. O thou vile king,
Give me my father!

Queen
     Calmly, good Laertes.   120

122 **cuckold:** betrayed husband.
123 **unsmirched:** unspotted, unstained.

128 **hedge:** surround.
129 **peep:** look at but from a distance.
130 **Acts little of his will:** cannot do what it would like to do.

141 **both the worlds:** this world and the next.
   give to negligence: consider unimportant.
143 **throughly:** thoroughly.

146 **husband:** manage.

Laertes

   That drop of blood that's calm proclaims me bastard;
   Cries cuckold to my father; brands the harlot
   Even here, between the chaste unsmirched brows
   Of my true mother.

King

                  What is the cause, Laertes,   125
   That thy rebellion looks so giant-like?
   Let him go, Gertrude; do not fear our person:
   There's such divinity doth hedge a king,
   That treason can but peep to what it would,
   Acts little of his will. Tell me, Laertes,   130
   Why thou art thus incens'd: let him go, Gertrude:
   Speak, man.

Laertes

   Where is my father?

King

             Dead.

Queen

                  But not by him.   135

King

   Let him demand his fill.

Laertes

   How came he dead? I'll not be juggled with:
   To hell, allegiance! vows, to the blackest devil!
   Conscience and grace, to the profoundest pit!
   I dare damnation: to this point I stand,   140
   That both the worlds I give to negligence,
   Let come what comes; only I'll be reveng'd
   Most throughly for my father.

King

                 Who shall stay you?

Laertes

   My will, not all the world: 145
   And for my means, I'll husband them so well,
   They shall go far with little.

151 **swoopstake:** sweepstake, all at once.

156 **pelican:** bird which in legend fed its young with its own blood.

157 **Repast:** feed.

159 **good child:** good son (without the modern implication of childishness).

161 **sensibly:** emotionally.

173 **fine:** refined, noble.

King

                              Good Laertes,
If you desire to know the certainty
Of your dear father's death, is 't writ in your revenge   150
That, swoopstake, you will draw both friend and foe,
Winner and loser?

Laertes

None but his enemies.

King

                              Will you know them then?

Laertes

To his good friends thus wide I'll ope my arms;   155
And, like the kind life-rend'ring pelican,
Repast them with my blood.

King

                              Why, now you speak
Like a good child and a true gentleman.
That I am guiltless of your father's death,   160
And am most sensibly in grief for it,
It shall as level to your judgment pierce
As day does to your eye.

Danes

                    [*Within*]   Let her come in.

Laertes

How now! what noise is that?   165

      Reenter Ophelia.

O heat, dry up my brains! tears seven times salt,
Burn out the sense and virtue of mine eye!
By heaven, thy madness shall be paid with weight,
Till our scale turn the beam. O rose of May!
Dear maid, kind sister, sweet Ophelia!   170
O heavens! is 't possible a young maid's wits
Should be as mortal as an old man's life?
Nature is fine in love, and where 'tis fine

174 **instance:** example.

183 **wheel:** the refrain of a song.
183–184 **false steward:** evidently a reference to a legend or ballad now lost.

185 **nothing's more than matter:** nonsense more eloquently effective than sense would be.

186 **rosemary:** This and other plants mentioned had symbolic meaning for the Elizabethans. Fennel, for example, symbolized flattery; rue, sorrow and repentance.

197 **bonnie sweet Robin:** reference to a ballad.

199 **favor:** charm.

It sends some precious instance of itself
After the thing it loves.   175

Ophelia
[*Sings*]   They bore him barefac'd on the bier:
            Hey non nonny, nonny, hey nonny:
            And in his grave rain'd many a tear—
Fare you well, my dove!

Laertes
Hadst thou thy wits, and didst persuade revenge,   180
It could not move thus.

Ophelia
You must sing down a-down, an you call him a-
down-a. O, how the wheel becomes it! It is the false
steward, that stole his master's daughter.

Laertes
This nothing's more than matter.   185

Ophelia
There's rosemary, that's for remembrance: pray you,
love, remember: and there is pansies, that's for
thoughts.

Laertes
A document in madness; thoughts and remembrance
fitted.   190

Ophelia
There's fennel for you, and columbines: there's rue
for you: and here's some for me: we may call it herb
of grace o' Sundays: O, you must wear your rue with
a difference. There's a daisy: I would give you some
violets, but they withered all when father died: they   195
say a' made a good end—
[*Sings*]   For bonnie sweet Robin is all my joy.

Laertes
Thought and affliction, passion, hell itself,
She turns to favor and to prettiness.

206 **poll:** head.

217 **collateral:** indirect.
218 **touched:** tinged with guilt.

226 **hatchment:** tablet with a coat of arms.
227 **ostentation:** ceremony.

Ophelia

  [*Sings*]   And will a' not come again?   200
            And will a' not come again?
               No, no, he is dead,
               Go to thy death-bed,
            He never will come again.
            His beard was as white as snow,   205
            All flaxen was his poll:
               He is gone, he is gone,
               And we cast away moan:
            God ha' mercy on his soul!

  And of all Christian souls, I pray God. God be wi'   210
  you.

                                  [*Exit.*

Laertes

  Do you see this, O God?

King

  Laertes, I must commune with your grief,
  Or you deny me right. Go but apart,
  Make choice of whom your wisest friends you will.   215
  And they shall hear and judge 'twixt you and me:
  If by direct or by collateral hand
  They find us touched, we will our kingdom give,
  Our crown, our life, and all that we call ours,
  To you in satisfaction; but if not,   220
  Be you content to lend your patience to us,
  And we shall jointly labor with your soul
  To give it due content.

Laertes

                Let this be so;
  His means of death, his obscure funeral,   225
  No trophy, sword, nor hatchment o'er his bones,
  No noble rite nor formal ostentation,
  Cry to be heard, as 'twere from heaven to earth,
  That I must call 't in question.

11 **let to know:** informed.

12 **overlooked:** looked over, perused.
13 **means:** means of access.

King

                       So you shall;   230
  And where th' offense is let the great axe fall.
  I pray you, go with me.

                                    [*Exeunt.*

Scene 6. *Another room in the castle*

Enter Horatio and a Servant.

Horatio

  What are they that would speak with me?

Servant

  Sea-faring men, sir: they say they have letters for you.

Horatio

  Let them come in.

                           [*Exit Servant.*
  I do not know from what part of the world
  I should be greeted, if not from Lord Hamlet.   5

  Enter Sailors.

First Sailor

  God bless you, sir.

Horatio

  Let him bless thee too.

First Sailor

  He shall, sir, an 't please him. There's a letter for
  you, sir; it comes from the ambassador that was
  bound for England; if your name be Horatio, as I am   10
  let to know it is.

Horatio

  [*Reads*] "Horatio, when thou shalt have overlooked
  this, give these fellows some means to the king: they

20 **thieves of mercy:** merciful thieves.

25 **bore:** importance.

1 **my acquittance seal:** clear me of wrongdoing.

have letters for him. Ere we were two days old at
sea, a pirate of very warlike appointment gave us   15
chase. Finding ourselves too slow of sail, we put on a
compelled valor, and in the grapple I boarded them:
on the instant they got clear of our ship; so I alone
became their prisoner. They have dealt with me like
thieves of mercy: but they knew what they did; I am   20
to do a good turn for them. Let the king have the
letters I have sent; and repair thou to me with as
much speed as thou wouldst fly death. I have words
to speak in thine ear will make thee dumb; yet are
they much too light for the bore of the matter. These   25
good fellows will bring thee where I am. Rosencrantz and Guildenstern hold their course for England: of them I have much to tell thee. Farewell.
  "He that thou knowest thine, Hamlet"
Come, I will make you way for these your letters;   30
And do 't the speedier, that you may direct me
To him from whom you brought them.
        [*Exeunt.*

Scene 7. *Another room in the castle*

Enter King and Laertes.

King
Now must your conscience my acquittance seal,
And you must put me in your heart for friend,
Sith you have heard, and with a knowing ear,
That he which hath your noble father slain
Pursued my life.   5
Laertes
     It well appears: but tell me
Why you proceeded not against these feats,

12 **unsinew'd:** weak.

16 **conjunctive:** closely joined.

20 **general gender:** common people.

22 **spring that turneth wood to stone:** spring with high lime content reputed to turn wood into stone.
23 **gyves:** shackles.
24 **slightly timber'd:** with shafts too light.

So crimeful and so capital in nature,
As by your safety, wisdom, all things else,
You mainly were stirr'd up.   10

King

                          O, for two special reasons,
Which may to you perhaps seem much unsinew'd,
But yet to me they're strong. The queen his mother
Lives almost by his looks; and for myself—
My virtue or my plague, be it either which—   15
She's so conjunctive to my life and soul,
That, as the star moves not but in his sphere,
I could not but by her. The other motive,
Why to a public count I might not go,
Is the great love the general gender bear him;   20
Who, dipping all his faults in their affection,
Would, like the spring that turneth wood to stone,
Convert his gyves to graces; so that my arrows,
Too slightly timber'd for so loud a wind,
Would have reverted to my bow again   25
And not where I had aim'd them.

Laertes

And so have I a noble father lost;
A sister driven into desp'rate terms,
Whose worth, if praises may go back again,
Stood challenger on mount of all the age   30
For her perfections: but my revenge will come.

King

Break not your sleeps for that: you must not think
That we are made of stuff so flat and dull
That we can let our beard be shook with danger
And think it pastime. You shortly shall hear more: 35
I lov'd your father, and we love ourself;
And that, I hope, will teach you to imagine—

Enter a Messenger, with letters.

How now! what news?

48 **naked:** unarmed, defenseless.

54 **abuse:** delusion.

55 **hand:** handwriting.

56 **character:** handwriting.

Messenger
>   Letters, my lord, from Hamlet:
This to your majesty; this to the queen.   40

King
From Hamlet! who brought them?

Messenger
Sailors, my lord, they say; I saw them not:
They were given me by Claudio; he receiv'd them
Of him that brought them.

King
>   Laertes, you shall hear them.   45
Leave us.
>   [*Exit Messenger.*
[*Reads*] "High and mighty, You shall know I am set
naked on your kingdom. Tomorrow shall I beg leave
to see your kingly eyes: when I shall, first asking
your pardon thereunto, recount the occasion of my   50
sudden and more strange return.
>   "Hamlet."
What should this mean? Are all the rest come back?
Or is it some abuse, and no such thing?

Laertes
Know you the hand?   55

King
'Tis Hamlet's character. "Naked"!
And in a postscript here, he says "alone."
Can you advise me?

Laertes
I'm lost in it, my lord. But let him come;
It warms the very sickness in my heart,   60
That I shall live and tell him to his teeth,
"Thus didest thou."

King
>   If it be so, Laertes—
As how should it be so? how otherwise?—
Will you be rul'd by me?   65

69 **checking:** balking (a term used in falconry).

71 **ripe in my device:** complete in my planning.

74 **uncharge the practice:** withhold an accusation.

85 **siege:** rank.

87 **riband:** ribbon, ornament.

89 **livery:** clothing, uniform.
90 **weeds:** robes.

94 **can well:** can perform well.
    gallant: valorous and courteous person.

Laertes
Aye, my lord;

So you will not o'errule me to a peace.

King

To thine own peace. If he be now return'd,
As checking at his voyage, and that he means
No more to undertake it, I will work him   70
To an exploit now ripe in my device,
Under the which he shall not choose but fall:
And for his death no wind of blame shall breathe;
But even his mother shall uncharge the practice,
And call it accident.   75

Laertes
My lord, I will be rul'd;

The rather, if you could devise it so
That I might be the organ.

King
It falls right.

You have been talk'd of since your travel much,   80
And that in Hamlet's hearing, for a quality
Wherein, they say, you shine: your sum of parts
Did not together pluck such envy from him,
As did that one, and that in my regard
Of the unworthiest siege.   85

Laertes
What part is that, my lord?

King

A very riband in the cap of youth,
Yet needful too; for youth no less becomes
The light and careless livery that it wears
Than settled age his sables and his weeds,   90
Importing health and graveness. Two months since,
Here was a gentleman of Normandy—
I've seen myself, and serv'd against, the French,
And they can well on horseback: but this gallant
Had witchcraft in 't; he grew unto his seat,   95

97 **incorps'd:** incorporate.

97–98 **demi-natured with the brave beast:** like a mythical centaur, half man, half horse.

99 **in forgery of shapes and tricks:** in thinking up feats.

103 **Lamond:** possibly a real person, Pietro Monte, called "Peter Mount" in English.

107 **made confession of you:** said that he knew you.

112 **scrimers:** fencers.

117 **play:** fence.

And to such wondrous doing brought his horse
As had he been incorps'd and demi-natured
With the brave beast: so far he topp'd my thought
That I, in forgery of shapes and tricks,
Come short of what he did.   100

Laertes

A Norman was 't?

King
A Norman.

Laertes
Upon my life, Lamond.

King

The very same.

Laertes
I know him well: he is the brooch indeed   105
And gem of all the nation.

King
He made confession of you,
And gave you such a masterly report,
For art and exercise in your defense,
And for your rapier most especial,   110
That he cried out, 'twould be a sight indeed
If one could match you: the scrimers of their nation,
He swore, had neither motion, guard, nor eye,
If you oppos'd them. Sir, this report of his
Did Hamlet so envenom with his envy   115
That he could nothing do but wish and beg
Your sudden coming o'er, to play with him.
Now, out of this—

Laertes

What out of this, my lord?

King
Laertes, was your father dear to you?   120
Or are you like the painting of a sorrow,
A face without a heart?

126 **passages of proof:** things that could prove it.

129 **abate:** lessen.
130 **still:** always.
131 **plurisy:** fullness, excess.

137 **quick o' the ulcer:** the heart of the grievance.

142 **sanctuarize:** make a sanctuary of.

146 **put on:** incite.

148 **in fine:** finally.
149 **remiss:** easygoing.

153 **unbated:** without the protective button at the tip.
pass of practice: treacherous thrust.

Laertes
                              Why ask you this?
King
  Not that I think you did not love your father,
  But that I know love is begun by time,   125
  And that I see, in passages of proof,
  Time qualifies the spark and fire of it.
  There lives within the very flame of love
  A kind of wick or snuff that will abate it;
  And nothing is at a like goodness still,   130
  For goodness, growing to a plurisy,
  Dies in his own too much: that we would do
  We should do when we would; for this "would"
          changes
  And hath abatements and delays as many
  As there are tongues, are hands, are accidents,   135
  And then this "should" is like a spendthrift sigh,
  That hurts by easing. But, to the quick o' the ulcer:
  Hamlet comes back: what would you undertake,
  To show yourself your father's son indeed
  More than in words?   140
Laertes
                      To cut his throat i' the church.
King
  No place indeed should murder sanctuarize;
  Revenge should have no bounds. But, good Laertes,
  Will you do this, keep close within your chamber.
  Hamlet return'd shall know you are come home: 145
  We'll put on those shall praise your excellence
  And set a double varnish on the fame
  The Frenchman gave you; bring you in fine together
  And wager on your heads: he, being remiss,
  Most generous and free from all contriving,   150
  Will not peruse the foils, so that with ease,
  Or with a little shuffling, you may choose
  A sword unbated, and in a pass of practice
  Requite him for your father.

157 **unction:** ointment, salve.
   mountebank: quack.
159 **cataplasm:** poultice.
160 **simples:** herbs.

163 **gall:** scratch, wound.

168 **drift:** plot, intentions.
169 **assay'd:** attempted.

172 **cunnings:** respective skill.

177 **chalice for the nonce:** cup for the occasion.
178 **stuck:** thrust.

Laertes

       I will do 't;　　　155
And for that purpose I'll anoint my sword.
I bought an unction of a mountebank,
So mortal that but dip a knife in it,
Where it draws blood no cataplasm so rare,
Collected from all simples that have virtue　　　160
Under the moon, can save the thing from death
That is but scratch'd withal: I'll touch my point
With this contagion, that, if I gall him slightly,
It may be death.

King

      Let's further think of this;　　　165
Weigh what convenience both of time and means
May fit us to our shape: if this should fail,
And that our drift look through our bad performance,
'Twere better not assay'd: therefore this project
Should have a back or second, that might hold　　　170
If this did blast in proof. Soft! let me see:
We'll make a solemn wager on your cunnings:
I ha 't:
When in your motion you are hot and dry—
As make your bouts more violent to that end—　　　175
And that he calls for drink, I'll have prepar'd him
A chalice for the nonce; whereon but sipping,
If he by chance escape your venom'd stuck,
Our purpose may hold there. But stay, what noise?

  Enter Queen

How now, sweet queen!　　　180

Queen

 One woe doth tread upon another's heel,
So fast they follow: your sister's drown'd, Laertes.

Laertes

 Drown'd! O, where?

Queen

 There is a willow grows aslant a brook,

185 **hoar leaves:**   white under side of leaves.

187 **long purples:**   a kind of flower.
188 **liberal:**   plain-spoken.

190 **pendent:**   overhanging.
coronet weeds: flower garlands.

196 **incapable of:**   insensible to, unable to realize.
197 **indued:**   suited.

200 **lay:**   song.

206 **trick:**   habit, way.

208 **the woman will be out:**   womanly weakness will be gone
with the tears.
209 **fain would:**   is ready to.
210 **douts:**   extinguishes.

That shows his hoar leaves in the glassy stream;　　185
There with fantastic garlands did she come
Of crow-flowers, nettles, daisies, and long purples,
That liberal shepherds give a grosser name,
But our cold maids do dead men's fingers call them:
There, on the pendent boughs her coronet weeds　　190
Clambering to hang, an envious sliver broke;
When down her weedy trophies and herself
Fell in the weeping brook. Her clothes spread wide,
And mermaid-like a while they bore her up:
Which time she chanted snatches of old tunes,　　195
As one incapable of her own distress,
Or like a creature native and indued
Unto that element: but long it could not be
Till that her garments, heavy with their drink,
Pull'd the poor wretch from her melodious lay　　200
To muddy death.

Laertes

　　　　　　Alas, then she is drown'd!

Queen
　Drown'd, drown'd.

Laertes
　To much of water hast thou, poor Ophelia,
　And therefore I forbid my tears: but yet　　205
　It is our trick; nature her custom holds,
　Let shame say what it will: when these are gone,
　The woman will be out. Adieu, my lord:
　I have a speech of fire that fain would blaze,
　But that this folly douts it.　　210

　　　　　　　　　　　　[*Exit.*

King
　　　　　　Let's follow, Gertrude:
　How much I had to do to calm his rage!
　Now fear I this will give it start again;
　Therefore let's follow.

　　　　　　　　　　[*Exeunt.*

1–2 **willfully seeks her own salvation:**   commits suicide.

4 **straight:**   straightway, at once.
  crowner: coroner.

9 **se offendendo:**   blunder for *se defendendo,* or *self-de-fense.*

12 **argal:**   blunder for *ergo,* Latin for *therefore.*

14 **delver:**   digger.

ACT V

Scene 1. A churchyard

Enter two Clowns, with spades, &c.

First Clown
Is she to be buried in Christian burial that willfully
seeks her own salvation?

Second Clown
I tell thee she is; and therefore make her grave
straight: the crowner hath sat on her, and finds it
Christian burial.   5

First Clown
How can that be, unless she drowned herself in her
own defense?

Second Clown
Why, 'tis found so.

First Clown
It must be "se offendendo"; it cannot be else. For
here lies the point: if I drown myself wittingly, it   10
argues an act: and an act hath three branches; it is,
to act, to do, to perform: argal, she drowned herself
wittingly.

Second Clown
Nay, but hear you, goodman delver.

First Clown
Give me leave. Here lies the water; good: here stands   15
the man; good: if the man go to this water and drown
himself, it is, will he, nill he, he goes; mark you that;
but if the water come to him and drown him, he
drowns not himself: argal, he that is not guilty of his
own death shortens not his own life.   20

22 **crowner's quest:** coroner's inquest.

27 **countenance:** favor, privilege.
28 **even:** fellow.

30 **hold up:** continue.

38–39 **confess thyself:** The saying concludes, "and be hanged."

Second Clown
　But is this law?

First Clown
　Aye, marry, is 't; crowner's quest law.

Second Clown
　Will you ha' the truth on 't? If this had not been a
　gentlewoman, she should have been buried out o'
　Christian burial.　　　　　　　　　　　　　　　　　25

First Clown
　Why, there thou say'st: and the more pity that great
　folk should have countenance in this world to drown
　or hang themselves, more than their even Christian.
　Come, my spade. There is no ancient gentlemen but
　gardeners, ditchers and grave-makers: they hold up　　30
　Adam's profession.

Second Clown
　Was he a gentleman?

First Clown
　A' was the first that ever bore arms.

Second Clown
　Why, he had none.

First Clown
　What, art a heathen? How dost thou understand the　　35
　Scripture? The Scripture says Adam digged: could he
　dig without arms? I'll put another question to thee:
　if thou answerest me not to the purpose, confess
　thyself—

Second Clown
　Go to.　　　　　　　　　　　　　　　　　　　　　　40

First Clown
　What is he that builds stronger than either the ma-
　son, the shipwright, or the carpenter?

Second Clown
　The gallows-maker; for that frame outlives a thousand
　tenants.

52 **unyoke:**   your day's work is done.

60 **Yaughan:**   probably the keeper of a famous alehouse near
the Globe.
stoup: drinking cup.

63 **behove:**   profit, advantage.

67 **property of easiness:**   indifference through habit.

First Clown

    I like thy wit well, in good faith: the gallows does   45
well; but how does it well? it does well to those that
do ill: now, thou dost ill to say the gallows is built
stronger than the church: argal, the gallows may do
well to thee. To 't again, come.

Second Clown

    "Who builds stronger than a mason, a shipwright, or   50
a carpenter?"

First Clown

    Aye, tell me that, and unyoke.

Second Clown

    Marry, now I can tell.

First Clown

    To 't.

Second Clown

    Mass, I cannot tell.   55

    Enter Hamlet and Horatio, afar off.

First Clown

    Cudgel thy brains no more about it, for your dull ass
will not mend his pace with beating, and when you
are asked this question next, say "a grave-maker:" the
houses that he makes last till doomsday. Go, get thee
to Yaughan; fetch me a stoup of liquor.   60

                    [*Exit Second Clown.*
                    [*He digs, and sings.*

    In youth, when I did love, did love,
        Methought it was very sweet,
    To contract, O, the time, for-a my behove,
        O, methought, there-a was nothing-a meet.

Hamlet

    Has this fellow no feeling of his business, that he   65
sings at grave-making?

Horatio

    Custom hath made it in him a property of easiness.

69 **daintier:** more delicate.

75 **jowls:** knocks.
76 **Cain's jaw-bone:** According to the Bible, Cain slew his brother Abel with the jawbone of an ass.

86 **chapless:** missing the lower jaw.
87 **mazzard:** skull.
88 **trick:** skill.

90 **loggats:** a game resembling bowls.

Hamlet
'Tis e'en so: the hand of little employment hath the
daintier sense.

First Clown
    [*Sings*]   But age, with his stealing steps,   70
                Hath claw'd me in his clutch,
                And hath shipped me intil the land,
                As if I had never been such.
                                [*Throws up a skull.*

Hamlet
That skull had a tongue in it, and could sing once:
how the knave jowls it to the ground, as if it were   75
Cain's jaw-bone, that did the first murder! It might
be the pate of a politician, which this ass now o'er-
reaches; one that would circumvent God, might it
not?

Horatio
It might, my lord.   80

Hamlet
Or of a courtier, which could say "Good morrow,
sweet lord! How dost thou, sweet lord?" This might
be my lord such-a-one, that praised my lord such-a-
one's horse, when he meant to beg it; might it not?

Horatio
Aye, my lord.   85

Hamlet
Why, e'en so: and now my Lady Worm's; chapless,
and knocked about the mazzard with a sexton's spade:
here's fine revolution, an we had the trick to see 't.
Did these bones cost no more the breeding, but to
play at loggats with 'em? mine ache to think on 't.   90

First Clown
    [*Sings*]   A pick-axe, and a spade, a spade,
                For and a shrouding sheet:

96 **quiddities:** subtleties.

  quillets: subtle arguments.

98 **sconce:** colloquial word for *head*.

99–100 **action of battery:** suit for assault.

107 **indentures:** contracts.

O, a pit of clay for to be made
For such a guest is meet.

                    [*Throws up another skull.*

Hamlet

There's another: why may not that be the skull of a   95
lawyer? Where be his quiddities now, his quillets, his
cases, his tenures, and his tricks? why does he suffer
this rude knave now to knock him about the sconce
with a dirty shovel, and will not tell him of his action
of battery? Hum! This fellow might be in 's time a   100
great buyer of land, with his statutes, his recognizances,
his fines, his double vouchers, his recoveries: is this
the fine of his fines and the recovery of his recoveries,
to have his fine pate full of fine dirt? will his vouchers vouch him no more of his purchases, and double   105
ones too, than the length and breadth of a pair of
indentures? The very conveyances of his lands will
hardly lie in this box; and must the inheritor himself
have no more, ha?

Horatio

Not a jot more, my lord.   110

Hamlet

Is not parchment made of sheep-skins?

Horatio

Aye, my lord, and of calf-skins too.

Hamlet

They are sheep and calves which seek out assurance in
that. I will speak to this fellow. Whose grave's this,
sirrah?   115

First Clown

Mine, sir.
        [*Sings*]   O, a pit of clay for to be made
                    For such a guest is meet.

Hamlet

I think it be thine indeed, for thou liest in 't.

132 **absolute:** positive, literal in his phraseology.
132–133 **speak by the card:** speak to the point.
133 **equivocation:** language with two possible interpretations.
135 **picked:** refined, fastidious.
136 **galls his kibe:** irritates the sore on his (the courtier's) heel by walking so close in imitation.

First Clown

    You lie out on 't, sir, and therefore 'tis not yours: for   120
    my part, I do not lie in 't, and yet it is mine.

Hamlet

    Thou dost lie in 't, to be in 't and say it is thine: 'tis
    for the dead, not for the quick; therefore thou liest.

First Clown

    'Tis a quick lie, sir; 'twill away again, from me to you.

Hamlet

    What man dost thou dig it for?   125

First Clown

    For no man, sir.

Hamlet

    What woman then?

First Clown

    For none neither.

Hamlet

    Who is to be buried in 't?

First Clown

    One that was a woman, sir; but, rest her soul, she's   130
    dead.

Hamlet

    How absolute the knave is! we must speak by the
    card, or equivocation will undo us. By the Lord, Ho-
    ratio, this three years I have taken note of it; the age
    is grown so picked that the toe of the peasant comes   135
    so near the heel of the courtier, he galls his kibe. How
    long hast thou been a grave-maker?

First Clown

    Of all the days i' the year, I came to 't that day that
    our last King Hamlet o'ercame Fortinbras.

Hamlet

    How long is that since?   140

First Clown

    Cannot you tell that? every fool can tell that: it was

159 **pocky:** diseased.
   corses: corpses.

that very day that young Hamlet was born: he that is
mad, and sent into England.

Hamlet

Aye, marry, why was he sent into England?

First Clown

Why, because a' was mad; a' shall recover his wits   145
there: or, if a' do not, 'tis no great matter there.

Hamlet

Why?

First Clown

'Twill not be seen in him there; there the men are as
mad as he.

Hamlet

How came he mad?   150

First Clown

Very strangely, they say.

Hamlet

How "strangely"?

First Clown

Faith, e'en with losing his wits.

Hamlet

Upon what ground?

First Clown

Why, here in Denmark: I have been sexton here, man   155
and boy, thirty years.

Hamlet

How long will a man lie i' the earth ere he rot?

First Clown

I' faith, if a' be not rotten before a' die—as we have
many pocky corses now-a-days, that will scarce hold
the laying in—a' will last you some eight year or nine   160
year: a tanner will last you nine year.

Hamlet

Why he more than another?

165 **whoreson:** term of humorous abuse.

173 **Rhenish:** Rhine wine.

186 **chop-fallen:** grisly pun on the fact that the skull is chin-less, chapfallen.
187 **favor:** appearance.

First Clown

Why, sir, his hide is so tanned with his trade that a'
will keep out water a great while; and your water is a
sore decayer of your whoreson dead body. Here's a   165
skull now: this skull has lain i' the earth three and
twenty years.

Hamlet

Whose was it?

First Clown

A whoreson mad fellow's it was: whose do you think
it was?   170

Hamlet

Nay, I know not.

First Clown

A pestilence on him for a mad rogue! a' poured a
flagon of Rhenish on my head once. This same skull,
sir, was Yorick's skull, the king's jester.

Hamlet

This?   175

First Clown

E'en that.

Hamlet

Let me see. [*Takes the skull.*]   Alas, poor Yorick!
I knew him, Horatio: a fellow of infinite jest, of most
excellent fancy: he hath borne me on his back a
thousand times; and now how abhorred in my imag-   180
ination it is! my gorge rises at it. Here hung those
lips that I have kissed I know not how oft. Where be
your gibes now? your gambols? your songs? your flashes
of merriment, that were wont to set the table on a
roar? Not one now, to mock your own grinning? quite   185
chop-fallen? Now get you to my lady's chamber, and
tell her, let her paint an inch thick, to this favor she
must come; make her laugh at that. Prithee, Horatio,
tell me one thing.

191 **Alexander:**   Alexander the Great of Macedon.

198 **bunghole:**   hole in barrel from which the liquid can pour.

209 **expel:**   keep out.

Horatio

What's that, my lord?   190

Hamlet

Dost thou think Alexander looked o' this fashion i'
the earth?

Horatio

E'en so.

Hamlet

And smelt so? pah!

                              [*Puts down the skull.*

Horatio

E'en so, my lord.   195

Hamlet

To what base uses we may return, Horatio! Why may
not imagination trace the noble dust of Alexander, till
he find it stopping a bunghole?

Horatio

'Twere to consider too curiously, to consider so.

Hamlet

No, faith, not a jot; but to follow him thither with   200
modesty enough and likelihood to lead it: as thus:
Alexander died, Alexander was buried, Alexander re-
turneth into dust; the dust is earth; of earth we make
loam; and why of that loam, whereto he was con-
verted, might they not stop a beer-barrel?   205

Imperious Cæsar, dead and turn'd to clay,
Might stop a hole to keep the wind away:
O, that that earth, which kept the world in awe,
Should patch a wall to expel the winter's flaw!

But soft! but soft! aside: here comes the king.   210

*Enter Priests &c., in procession; the Corpse of
Ophelia, Laertes, and Mourners following; King,
Queen, their trains, &c.*

The queen, the courtiers: who is this they follow?

212 **maimed:**   imperfect, incomplete.
    betoken: indicate.
214 **Fordo its own life:**   commit suicide.
    of some estate: of high rank.
215 **couch:**   hide.

220 **warranty:**   justification, permission.

224 **shards:**   bits of pottery.
225 **crants:**   funeral garlands.
226 **strewments:**   strewing of flowers over the grave.

And with such maimed rites? This doth betoken
The corse they follow did with desp'rate hand
Fordo its own life: 'twas of some estate.
Couch we awhile, and mark.   215
                        [*Retiring with Horatio.*

Laertes
What ceremony else?

Hamlet
That is Laertes, a very noble youth: mark.

Laertes
What ceremony else?

First Priest
Her obsequies have been as far enlarg'd
As we have warranty: her death was doubtful;   220
And, but that great command o'ersways the order
She should in ground unsanctified have lodg'd
Till the last trumpet; for charitable prayers,
Shards, flints and pebbles should be thrown on her:
Yet here she is allow'd her virgin crants,   225
Her maiden strewments and the bringing home
Of bell and burial.

Laertes
Must there no more be done?

First Priest
                        No more be done:
We should profane the service of the dead   230
To sing a requiem and such rest to her
As to peace-parted souls.

Laertes
                        Lay her i' the earth:
And from her fair and unpolluted flesh
May violets spring! I tell thee, churlish priest,   235
A minist'ring angel shall my sister be,
When thou liest howling.

Hamlet
                        What, the fair Ophelia!

245 **ingenious:** intelligent, conscious.

250 **Pelion:** In mythology the giants piled the mountain Ossa on another high mountain, Pelion, in a futile effort to reach the stronghold of the gods, whom they were fighting.
251 **Olympus:** high mountain in Greece, legendary home of the gods.
254 **wandering stars:** planets. (*Planet* comes from a Greek word meaning "wanderer.")

260 **splenitive:** filled with spleen; impetuous and hot-headed.

Queen
  [*Scattering flowers.*]   Sweets to the sweet: farewell!
  I hop'd thou shouldst have been my Hamlet's wife;   240
  I thought thy bride-bed to have deck'd, sweet maid,
  And not have strew'd thy grave.
Laertes
                              O, treble woe
  Fall ten times treble on that cursed head
  Whose wicked deed thy most ingenious sense   245
  Depriv'd thee of! Hold off the earth awhile,
  Till I have caught her once more in mine arms:
                              [*Leaps into the grave.*
  Now pile your dust upon the quick and dead,
  Till of this flat a mountain you have made
  To o'ertop old Pelion or the skyish head   250
  Of blue Olympus.
Hamlet
  [*Advancing*]   What is he whose grief
  Bears such an emphasis? whose phrase of sorrow
  Conjures the wandering stars and makes them stand
  Like wonder-wounded hearers? This is I,   255
  Hamlet the Dane.
                              [*Leaps into the grave.*

Laertes
  The devil take thy soul!
                              [*Grappling with him.*
Hamlet
                              Thou pray'st not well.
  I prithee, take thy fingers from my throat;
  For, though I am not splenitive and rash,   260
  Yet have I in me something dangerous,
  Which let thy wisdom fear. Hold off thy hand.
King
  Pluck them asunder.
Queen
                              Hamlet, Hamlet!

268 **wag:** open and shut.

275 **'Swounds:** God's wounds (an oath).
276 **Woo't:** would you.

277 **eisel:** vinegar, symbol of a bitter drink.

280 **quick:** alive.

283 **burning zone:** pathway of the sun.

284 **Ossa:** Hamlet throws Laertes' boast back in his face. See note 250 above.
mouth: talk exaggeratedly and wildly.

All

Gentlemen—   265

Horatio

Good my lord, be quiet.

[*The Attendants part them, and they come
out of the grave.*

Hamlet

Why, I will fight with him upon this theme
Until my eyelids will no longer wag.

Queen

O my son, what theme?

Hamlet

I lov'd Ophelia: forty thousand brothers   270
Could not, with all their quantity of love,
Make up my sum. What wilt thou do for her?

King

O, he is mad, Laertes.

Queen

For love of God, forbear him.

Hamlet

'Swounds, show me what thou 'lt do: 275
Woo't weep? woo't fight? woo't fast? woo't tear thy-
self?
Woo't drink up eisel? eat a crocodile?
I'll do 't. Dost thou come here to whine?
To outface me with leaping in her grave?
Be buried quick with her, and so will I: 280
And, if thou prate of mountains, let them throw
Millions of acres on us, till our ground,
Singeing his pate against the burning zone,
Make Ossa like a wart! Nay, an thou 'lt mouth,
I'll rant as well as thou.   285

Queen

This is mere madness:
And thus a while the fit will work on him;

289 **golden couplets:** two young birds.

300 **living:** lasting.

 Anon, as patient as the female dove
 When that her golden couplets are disclos'd,
 His silence will sit drooping.   290

Hamlet
       Hear you, sir;
 What is the reason that you use me thus?
 I lov'd you ever: but it is no matter;
 Let Hercules himself do what he may,
 The cat will mew, and dog will have his day. 295
            [*Exit.*

King
 I pray thee, good Horatio, wait upon him.
         [*Exit Horatio.*
 [*To Laertes*] Strengthen your patience in our last
  night's speech;
 We'll put the matter to the present push.
 Good Gertrude, set some watch over your son.
 This grave shall have a living monument: 300
 An hour of quiet shortly shall we see;
 Till then, in patience our proceeding be.
         [*Exeunt.*

Scene 2. A *hall in the castle*

Enter Hamlet and Horatio.

Hamlet
 So much for this, sir: now shall you see the other;
 You do remember all the circumstance?

Horatio
 Remember it, my lord!

Hamlet
 Sir, in my heart there was a kind of fighting,

6 **mutines:** mutineers.
  bilboes: fetters for a ship's prisoners.

9 **pall:** fail. (Impulsive action sometimes succeeds where careful plans fail.)

15 **them:** Rosencrantz and Guildenstern.

21 **larded:** garnished.
22 **importing:** concerning.
23 **bugs and goblins:** evils.
   in my life: in my continuing to live.
24 **on the supervise:** immediately upon reading.
   no leisure bated: no delay permitted.

32 **make a prologue to my brains:** begin to think.
33 **They had begun the play:** my mind began to concoct a plan.
34 **fair:** legibly, in a fine script.

That would not let me sleep: methought I lay   5
Worse than the mutines in the bilboes. Rashly,
And prais'd be rashness for it, let us know,
Our indiscretion sometime serves us well
When our deep plots do pall; and that should learn us
There's a divinity that shapes our ends,   10
Rough-hew them how we will.

Horatio

                    That is most certain.

Hamlet

Up from my cabin,
My sea-gown scarf'd about me, in the dark
Grop'd I to find out them; had my desire,   15
Finger'd their packet, and in fine withdrew
To mine own room again; making so bold,
My fears forgetting manners, to unseal
Their grand commission; where I found, Horatio—
O royal knavery!—an exact command,   20
Larded with many several sorts of reasons,
Importing Denmark's health and England's too,
With, ho! such bugs and goblins in my life,
That, on the supervise, no leisure bated,
No, not to stay the grinding of the axe,   25
My head should be struck off.

Horatio

                    Is 't possible?

Hamlet

Here's the commission: read it at more leisure,
But wilt thou hear now how I did proceed?

Horatio

I beseech you.   30

Hamlet

Being thus be-netted round with villainies—
Or I could make a prologue to my brains,
They had begun the play—I sat me down;
Devis'd a new commission; wrote it fair:

35 **statists:** statesmen. (Hamlet once cultivated bad handwriting as a kind of achievement!)

38 **did me yeoman's service:** helped me a great deal.

41 **conjuration:** strong request.

45 **comma:** connection.
amities: friendship.

48 **debatement:** discussion.

50 **shriving-time:** time for confession and absolution.

52 **ordinant:** ordaining, guiding.

56 **Subscrib'd it:** signed it.
gave 't the impression: sealed it.
57 **changeling:** substituted message.
known: recognized, realized.
58 **sequent:** following.

60 **go to 't:** go to their deaths.

63 **insinuation:** meddling.

I once did hold it, as our statists do,   35
A baseness to write fair, and labor'd much
How to forget that learning; but, sir, now
It did me yeoman's service: wilt thou know
Th' effect of what I wrote?

Horatio

                                        Aye, good my lord.   40

Hamlet

An earnest conjuration from the king,
As England was his faithful tributary,
As love between them like the palm might flourish,
As peace should still her wheaten garland wear
And stand a comma 'tween their amities,   45
And many such-like as's of great charge,
That, on the view and knowing of these contents,
Without debatement further, more or less,
He should the bearers put to sudden death,
Not shriving-time allow'd.   50

Horatio

                        How was this seal'd?

Hamlet

Why, even in that was heaven ordinant.
I had my father's signet in my purse,
Which was the model of that Danish seal:
Folded the writ up in the form of th' other;   55
Subscrib'd it; gave 't the impression; plac'd it safely,
The changeling never known. Now, the next day
Was our sea-fight; and what to this was sequent
Thou know'st already.

Horatio

So Guildenstern and Rosencrantz go to 't.   60

Hamlet

Why, man, they did make love to this employment;
They are not near my conscience; their defeat
Does by their own insinuation grow:

65 **pass:** thrust.
   fell: deadly.

71 **proper:** own, very.
72 **cozenage:** deceit, trickery.

74 **canker of our nature:** this source of corruption.

79 **say "One":** count to *one*.

84 **bravery:** showiness, ostentation.

88 **water-fly:** a showy do-nothing, a trifler.

'Tis dangerous when the baser nature comes
Between the pass and fell incensed points　　　　65
Of mighty opposites.

Horatio

　　　　　　　　　　Why, what a king is this!

Hamlet

Does it not, think'st thee, stand me now upon—
He that hath kill'd my king, an whor'd my mother;
Popp'd in between th' election and my hopes;　　　　70
Thrown out his angle for my proper life,
And with such cozenage—is 't not perfect conscience,
To quit him with this arm? and is 't not to be damn'd,
To let this canker of our nature come
In further evil?　　　　75

Horatio

It must be shortly known to him from England
What is the issue of the business there.

Hamlet

It will be short: the interim is mine;
And a man's life's no more than to say "One."
But I am very sorry, good Horatio,　　　　80
That to Laertes I forgot myself;
For, by the image of my cause, I see
The portraiture of his: I'll court his favors:
But, sure, the bravery of his grief did put me
Into a towering passion.　　　　85

Horatio

　　　　　　　　Peace! who comes here?

　　　Enter Osric.

Osric

Your lordship is right welcome back to Denmark.

Hamlet

I humbly thank you, sir. Dost know this water-fly?

Horatio

No, my good lord.

92 **crib:** manger.
92–93 **king's mess:** king's feasting.
93 **chough:** chattering crow.

101 **indifferent:** somewhat, rather.

109 **for mine ease:** roughly equivalent here to "please, for my sake."
111 **absolute:** perfect, faultless.
differences: distinguishing qualities.
112 **soft society:** courteous manner.
great showing: fine appearance.

Hamlet

Thy state is the more gracious, for 'tis a vice to know   90
him. He hath much land, and fertile: let a beast be
lord of beasts, and his crib shall stand at the king's
mess: 'tis a chough, but, as I say, spacious in the pos-
session of dirt.

Osric

Sweet lord, if your lordship were at leisure, I should   95
impart a thing to you from his majesty.

Hamlet

I will receive it, sir, with all diligence of spirit. Put
your bonnet to his right use; 'tis for the head.

Osric

I thank your lordship, it is very hot.

Hamlet

No, believe me, 'tis very cold; the wind is northerly.   100

Osric

It is indifferent cold, my lord, indeed.

Hamlet

But yet methinks it is very sultry and hot, or my complexion—

Osric

Exceedingly, my lord; it is very sultry, as 'twere—I
cannot tell how. But, my lord, his majesty bade me   105
signify to you that he has laid a great wager on your
head: sir, this is the matter—

Hamlet

I beseech you, remember—

                    [*Hamlet moves him to put on his hat.*

Osric

Nay, good my lord; for mine ease, in good faith. Sir,
here is newly come to court Laertes; believe me, an   110
absolute gentleman, full of most excellent differences,
of very soft society and great showing: indeed, to
speak feelingly of him, he is the card or calendar of

113–114 **card or calendar of gentry:** a model of courtesy.
114 **continent of:** inventory, sum.

116 **definement:** definition, description.
   perdition: loss.
118 **yaw:** move erratically (a sailing term).
118–119 **in respect of his quick sail:** in the rapid telling of his attainments. (Hamlet here mocks Osric's extravagant praise of Laertes and imitates Osric's style as he does so.)
120 **a soul of great article:** a soul with so many qualities that its inventory would be very large.
121 **infusion:** qualities.
   dearth: scarceness.
122 **semblable:** equal, true image.
123 **umbrage:** shadow.
125 **concernancy:** import, meaning.

137 **approve:** commend.

gentry, for you shall find in him the continent of what
part a gentleman would see.   115

Hamlet

Sir, his definement suffers no perdition in you; though,
I know, to divide him inventorially would dizzy the
arithmetic of memory, and yet but yaw neither, in
respect of his quick sail. But in the verity of extol-
ment, I take him to be a soul of great article, and his   120
infusion of such dearth and rareness, as, to make true
diction of him, his semblable is his mirror, and who
else would trace him, his umbrage, nothing more.

Osric

Your lordship speaks most infallibly of him.

Hamlet

The concernancy, sir? why do we wrap the gentleman   125
in our more rawer breath?

Osric

Sir?

Horatio

Is 't not possible to understand in another tongue?
You will do 't, sir, really.

Hamlet

What imports the nomination of this gentleman?   130

Osric

Of Laertes?

Horatio

His purse is empty already; all 's golden words are
spent.

Hamlet

Of him, sir.

Osric

I know you are not ignorant—   135

Hamlet

I would you did, sir; yet, in faith, if you did, it would
not much approve me. Well, sir?

142 **imputation:** reputation.
143 **meed:** merit.
   unfellowed: unequaled.

148 **imponed:** staked.
149 **poniards:** daggers.
   assigns: accessories.
150 **girdle:** sword belt.
   hanger: strap.
   carriages: hangers, straps.
151 **responsive:** corresponding in appearance or design.
152 **liberal conceit:** imaginative design.

154 **margent:** margin, marginal interpretation.

157 **germane:** relevant.

Osric

You are not ignorant of what excellence Laertes is—

Hamlet

I dare not confess that, lest I should compare with
him in excellence; but, to know a man well, were to   140
know himself.

Osric

I mean, sir, for his weapon; but in the imputation laid
on him by them, in his meed he's unfellowed.

Hamlet

What's his weapon?

Osric

Rapier and dagger.   145

Hamlet

That's two of his weapons: but, well.

Osric

The king, sir, hath wagered with him six Barbary
horses: against the which he has imponed, as I take
it, six French rapiers and poniards, with their assigns,
as girdle, hanger, and so: three of the carriages, in   150
faith, are very dear to fancy, very responsive to the
hilts, most delicate carriages, and of very liberal conceit.

Hamlet

What call you the carriages?

Horatio

I knew you must be edified by the margent ere you
had done.   155

Osric

The carriages, sir, are the hangers.

Hamlet

The phrase would be more germane to the matter if
we could carry a cannon by our sides: I would it
might be hangers till then. But, on: six Barbary horses
against six French swords, their assigns, and three lib- 160

163 **passes:** dueling bouts.

167 **vouchsafe the answer:** agree to the arrangements.

169 **the opposition of your person in trial:** your participation in the match.

171 **breathing time:** time for exercise.

179 **for 's turn:** to do the job for him.

180 **lapwing:** bird that reputedly runs away when barely hatched.

180 **shell:** Osric's hat.

181 **comply:** observe full courtesy.
    dug: mother's breast.

183 **drossy:** worthless.

184 **outward habit of encounter:** superficial observance of social niceties.
    yesty: foamy, frothy.

eral-conceited carriages; that's the French bet against
the Danish. Why is this "imponed," as you call it?

Osric

The king, sir, hath laid, sir, that in a dozen passes
between yourself and him, he shall not exceed you
three hits: he hath laid on twelve for nine; and it   165
would come to immediate trial if your lordship would
vouchsafe the answer.

Hamlet

How if I answer "no"?

Osric

I mean, my lord, the opposition of your person in trial.

Hamlet

Sir, I will walk here in the hall: if it please his majesty,   170
it is the breathing time of day with me; let the foils be
brought, the gentleman willing, and the king hold his
purpose, I will win for him an I can; if not, I will gain
nothing but my shame and the odd hits.

Osric

Shall I redeliver you e'en so?   175

Hamlet

To this effect, sir, after what flourish your nature will.

Osric

I commend my duty to your lordship.

Hamlet

Yours, yours. [Exit Osric.] He does well to commend it himself; there are no tongues else for 's turn.

Horatio

This lapwing runs away with the shell on his head.   180

Hamlet

He did comply with his dug before he sucked it. Thus
has he—and many more of the same breed that I know
the drossy age dotes on—only got the tune of the
time and outward habit of encounter; a kind of yesty
collection, which carries them through and through   185

186 **fond and winnowed:** foolish and over-refined.

193 **fitness:** convenience.

197 **gentle entertainment:** show of kindness.

206 **gain-giving:** misgiving.

the most fond and winnowed opinions; and do but
blow them to their trial, the bubbles are out.

Enter a Lord.

Lord

My lord, his majesty commended him to you by young
Osric, who brings back to him, that you attend him in
the hall: he sends to know if your pleasure hold to   190
play with Laertes, or that you will take longer time.

Hamlet

I am constant to my purposes; they follow the king's
pleasure: if his fitness speaks, mine is ready; now or
whensoever, provided I be so able as now.

Lord

The king and queen and all are coming down.   195

Hamlet

In happy time.

Lord

The queen desires you to use some gentle entertainment to Laertes before you fall to play.

Hamlet

She well instructs me.

[Exit Lord.

Horatio

You will lose this wager, my lord.   200

Hamlet

I do not think so; since he went into France, I have
been in continual practice; I shall win at the odds.
But thou wouldst not think how ill all's here about
my heart: but it is no matter.

Horatio

Nay, good my lord—   205

Hamlet

It is but foolery; but it is such a kind of gain-giving
as would perhaps trouble a woman.

208–209 **forestall their repair:** tell them not to come.

210 **augury:** omens.

214 **aught:** anything at all.
215 **betimes:** early.

219 **presence:** people present.

Horatio

　If your mind dislike anything, obey it. I will forestall
　their repair hither, and say you are not fit.

Hamlet

　Not a whit; we defy augury: there is special provi-　　210
　dence in the fall of a sparrow. If it be now, 'tis not
　to come; if it be not to come, it will be now; if it be
　not now, yet it will come: the readiness is all; since
　no man has aught of what he leaves, what is 't to
　leave betimes? Let be.　　　　　　　　　　　　215

　　Enter King, Queen, Laertes, and Lords, Osric, and
　　other Attendants with foils and gauntlets; a table
　　and flagons of wine on it.

King

　Come, Hamlet, come, and take this hand from me.
　　　　　[*The King puts Laertes' hand into Hamlet's.*

Hamlet

　Give me your pardon, sir: I've done you wrong;
　But pardon 't, as you are a gentleman.
　This presence knows,
　And you must needs have heard, how I am punish'd　220
　With sore distraction. What I have done,
　That might your nature, honor and exception
　Roughly awake, I here proclaim was madness.
　Was 't Hamlet wrong'd Laertes? Never Hamlet:
　If Hamlet from himself be ta'en away,　　　　　225
　And when he's not himself does wrong Laertes,
　Then Hamlet does it not, Hamlet denies it.
　Who does it then? His madness: if 't be so,
　Hamlet is of the faction that is wrong'd;
　His madness is poor Hamlet's enemy.　　　　　230
　Sir, in this audience,
　Let my disclaiming from a purpos'd evil
　Free me so far in your most generous thoughts,
　That I have shot mine arrow o'er the house,
　And hurt my brother.　　　　　　　　　　　235

236 **satisfied in nature:** natural feelings are satisfied.

242 **ungor'd:** unwounded, unstained.

251 **Stick fiery off:** shine brightly.

259 **better'd:** improved.

Laertes
                    I am satisfied in nature,
Whose motive, in this case, should stir me most
To my revenge: but in my terms of honor
I stand aloof, and will no reconcilement,
Till by some elder masters of known honor   240
I have a voice and precedent of peace,
To keep my name ungor'd. But till that time
I do receive your offer'd love like love
And will not wrong it.

Hamlet
                    I embrace it freely,   245
And will this brother's wager frankly play.
Give us the foils. Come on.

Laertes
                    Come, one for me.

Hamlet
I'll be your foil, Laertes: in mine ignorance
Your skill shall, like a star i' the darkest night,   250
Stick fiery off indeed.

Laertes
                    You mock me, sir.

Hamlet
No, by this hand.

King
Give them the foils, young Osric. Cousin Hamlet,
You know the wager?   255

Hamlet
                    Very well, my lord;
Your grace has laid the odds o' the weaker side.

King
I do not fear it; I have seen you both:
But since he is better'd, we have therefore odds.

Laertes
This is too heavy; let me see another.   260

263 **stoups:** cups.

265 **quit:** requite, repay.
266 **ordnance:** cannon.

268 **union:** fine pearl.

271 **kettle:** kettledrum.

281 **palpable:** evident.

Hamlet
This likes me well. These foils have all a length?
                     [*They prepare to play.*

Osric
Aye, my good lord.

King
Set me the stoups of wine upon that table.
If Hamlet give the first or second hit,
Or quit in answer of the third exchange,   265
Let all the battlements their ordnance fire;
The king shall drink to Hamlet's better breath;
And in the cup an union shall he throw,
Richer than that which four successive kings
In Denmark's crown have worn. Give me the cups;   270
And let the kettle to the trumpet speak,
The trumpet to the cannoneer without,
The cannons to the heavens, the heaven to earth,
"Now the king drinks to Hamlet." Come, begin;
And you, the judges, bear a wary eye.   275

Hamlet
Come on, sir.

Laertes
               Come, my lord.
                          [*They play.*

Hamlet
                  One.

Laertes
                    No.

Hamlet
                     Judgment.   280

Osric
A hit, a very palpable hit.

Laertes
                 Well; again.

290 **fat and scant of breath:**   out of training.

292 **carouses:**   drinks.

King

Stay; give me drink. Hamlet, this pearl is thine;
Here's to thy health.

> [*Trumpets sound, and cannon shot off within.*
> Give him the cup.   285

Hamlet

I'll play this bout first; set it by awhile.
Come. [*They play.*] Another hit; what say you?

Laertes

A touch, a touch, I do confess 't.

King

Our son shall win.

Queen

> He's fat and scant of breath.   290
Here, Hamlet, take my napkin, rub thy brows:
The queen carouses to thy fortune, Hamlet.

Hamlet

Good madam!

King

> Gertrude, do not drink.

Queen

I will, my lord; I pray you, pardon me.   295

King

[*Aside*] It is the poison'd cup; it is too late.

Hamlet

I dare not drink yet, madam; by and by.

Queen

Come, let me wipe thy face.

Laertes

My lord, I'll hit him now.

King

> I do not think 't.   300

Laertes

[*Aside*] And yet it is almost against my conscience.

304 **make a wanton of me:**   merely play with me.

313 **springe:**   snare.

316 **swounds:**   faints.

Hamlet
  Come, for the third, Laertes: you but dally;
  I pray you, pass with your best violence;
  I am afeard you make a wanton of me.

Laertes
  Say you so? come on.   305

                                    [*They play.*

Osric
  Nothing, neither way.

Laertes
  Have at you now!
          [*Laertes wounds Hamlet; then, in scuffling, they
              change rapiers, and Hamlet wounds Laertes.*

King
                  Part them; they are incens'd.

Hamlet
  Nay, come, again.
                                  [*The Queen falls.*

Osric
                  Look to the queen there, ho!   310

Horatio
  They bleed on both sides. How is it, my lord?

Osric
  How is 't, Laertes?

Laertes
  Why, as a woodcock to mine own springe, Osric;
  I am justly kill'd with mine own treachery.

Hamlet
  How does the queen?   315

King
                  She swounds to see them bleed.

Queen
  No, no, the drink, the drink—O my dear Hamlet—
  The drink, the drink! I am poison'd.
                                          [*Dies.*

325 **unbated:** without the protective button at the tip.
envenom'd: poisoned.
practice: plot.

334 **union:** possible pun on *union* (pearl) and *union* (a join-ing).

337 **temper'd:** compounded.

Hamlet

   O villainy! Ho! let the door be lock'd:
   Treachery! seek it out.   320

                       [*Laertes falls.*

Laertes

   It is here, Hamlet: Hamlet, thou art slain;
   No medicine in the world can do thee good,
   In thee there is not half an hour of life;
   The treacherous instrument is in thy hand,
   Unbated and envenom'd: the foul practice   325
   Hath turn'd itself on me; lo, here I lie,
   Never to rise again: thy mother's poison'd:
   I can no more: the king, the king's to blame.

Hamlet

   The point envenom'd too!
   Then, venom, to thy work.   330

                      [*Stabs the King.*

All

   Treason! treason!

King

   O, yet defend me, friends; I am but hurt.

Hamlet

   Here, thou incestuous, murderous, damned Dane,
   Drink off this potion: is thy union here?
   Follow my mother.   335

                      [*King dies.*

Laertes

              He is justly serv'd;
   It is a poison temper'd by himself.
   Exchange forgiveness with me, noble Hamlet:
   Mine and my father's death come not upon thee,
   Nor thine on me!   340

                      [*Dies.*

Hamlet

   Heaven make thee free of it! I follow thee.
   I am dead, Horatio. Wretched queen, adieu!

345 **fell:**   cruel.

351 **antique Roman:**   The ancient Romans often preferred suicide to disgrace.

366 **o'er-crows:**   crows over, as in exultation.

369 **voice:**   vote.
370 **occurrents:**   occurrences.
371 **solicited:**   urged, moved, brought about (the occurrences).

You that look pale and tremble at this chance,
That are but mutes or audience to this act,
Had I but time—as this fell sergeant, death,   345
Is strict in his arrest—O, I could tell you—
But let it be. Horatio, I am dead;
Thou liv'st; report me and my cause aright
To the unsatisfied.

Horatio
                    Never believe it.   350
I am more an antique Roman than a Dane:
Here's yet some liquor left.

Hamlet
                    As thou 'rt a man,
Give me the cup: let go; by heaven, I'll ha 't.
O good Horatio, what a wounded name,   355
Things standing thus unknown, shall live behind me!
If thou didst ever hold me in thy heart,
Absent thee from felicity awhile,
And in this harsh world draw thy breath in pain,
To tell my story.   360
          [*March afar off, and shot within.*
What warlike noise is this?

Osric
Young Fortinbras, with conquest come from Poland,
To the ambassadors of England gives
This warlike volley.

Hamlet
                    O, I die, Horatio;   365
The potent poison quite o'er-crows my spirit:
I cannot live to hear the news from England;
But I do prophesy th' election lights
On Fortinbras: he has my dying voice;
So tell him, with the occurrents, more and less,   370
Which have solicited. The rest is silence.
                              [*Dies.*

378 **quarry:**   pile of bodies.

391 **jump:**   quickly.

397 **carnal:**   sensual.

Horatio
　　Now cracks a noble heart. Good night, sweet prince,
　　And flights of angels sing thee to thy rest!
　　　　　　　　　　　　　　　　　　　　　　[*March within.*
　　Why does the drum come hither?

　　　　Enter Fortinbras, and the English Ambassadors,
　　　　with drum, colors, and Attendants.

Fortinbras
　　Where is this sight?   375
Horatio
　　　　　　　　　　What is it you would see?
　　If aught of woe or wonder, cease your search.
Fortinbras
　　This quarry cries on havoc. O proud death,
　　What feast is toward in thine eternal cell,
　　That thou so many princes at a shot   380
　　So bloodily hast struck?
First Ambassador
　　　　　　　　　　　The sight is dismal;
　　And our affairs from England come too late:
　　The ears are senseless that should give us hearing,
　　To tell him his commandment is fulfill'd,   385
　　That Rosencrantz and Guildenstern are dead:
　　Where should we have our thanks?
Horatio
　　　　　　　　　　　　　　Not from his mouth
　　Had it th' ability of life to thank you:
　　He never gave commandment for their death.   390
　　But since, so jump upon this bloody question,
　　You from the Polack wars, and you from England,
　　Are here arriv'd, give order that these bodies
　　High on a stage be placed to the view;
　　And let me speak to the yet unknowing world   395
　　How these things came about: so shall you hear
　　Of carnal, bloody and unnatural acts,

406 **rights of memory:** remembered rights or claims.

409 **his mouth:** Hamlet's endorsement of Fortinbras.
410 **presently:** immediately.
411 **wild:** upset, disturbed.

416 **passage:** death.

420 **shows much amiss:** looks out of place.

Of accidental judgments, casual slaughters,
Of deaths put on by cunning and forc'd cause,
And, in this upshot, purposes mistook   400
Fall'n on th' inventors' heads: all this can I
Truly deliver.

Fortinbras
          Let us haste to hear it,
And call the noblest to the audience.
For me, with sorrow I embrace my fortune: 405
I have some rights of memory in this kingdom,
Which now to claim my vantage doth invite me.

Horatio
Of that I shall have also cause to speak,
And from his mouth whose voice will draw on more:
But let this same be presently perform'd,   410
Even while men's minds are wild; lest more mischance
On plots and errors happen.

Fortinbras
                    Let four captains
Bear Hamlet, like a soldier, to the stage;
For he was likely, had he been put on,   415
To have prov'd most royally: and, for his passage,
The soldiers' music and the rites of war
Speak loudly for him.
Take up the bodies: such a sight as this
Becomes the field, but here shows much amiss.   420
Go, bid the soldiers shoot.
          [*A dead march. Exeunt, bearing off the bodies:*
               after which a peal of ordnance is shot off.

READER'S GUIDE

Henry I. Christ

INTRODUCTION

If you were asked to name the world's most famous play, you would undoubtedly say *Hamlet*. Every great actor, it is said, secretly hopes to play Hamlet some day before he is too old. Perhaps every stage designer has, in the deepest recesses of his mind, some ideas for staging *Hamlet* in a way never seen before. Perhaps every director thinks about how *he* would present a *Hamlet* never done before.

Why not? The play is an eternal challenge, a lock with many keys, none of which ever fits perfectly. Every interpretation presents just a portion of the possibilities. Every new version opens up new vistas, without limiting further experimentation. Every generation comes, looks, and studies the play, but never comes up with all the answers.

Hamlet has been presented in dozens of ways, from the most elaborately costumed production to one in modern dress. It has been put on as though it were a major rehearsal before opening night. It has been located in some mythical nineteenth-century country. It has been set in a modern dictatorship, with the king a murderous strong man of a decadent country.

The role of Hamlet has been attempted by young men and old men, by women as well as men, by the most celebrated actors of their day and by obscure performers who brought a freshness and naiveté to the part. The lines have been analyzed and sifted for centuries, and each actor has wrestled with the basic motivation of the young hero. Doubtless, centuries hence, in an age we cannot even visualize, on stages whose nature we cannot possibly predict, actors will still be struggling with the most challenging role of all, that of Hamlet.

You surely have heard much about *Hamlet* before coming to it now. You may have developed certain prejudices and have acquired certain misinformation. Try to read the play now with a fresh eye and an open mind. Try to find the answer for yourself to the eternal question of Hamlet's actions. If *Hamlet* is a reflection of every man, then every individual man must somehow decide for himself just what moves Hamlet, through delay and despair, to ultimate revenge and death.

In the *Reader's Guide*, for each scene you will face certain questions grouped around these major topics:

1. Plot
2. Characterization
3. Staging and Directing
4. Interpretation
5. Language and Imagery

Before beginning your reading of the book and your work with the questions, read the following explanatory comments on each of these five topics.

PLOT

Just as a story, *Hamlet* makes for exciting reading. There are intrigues, misunderstandings, murders. The action stops briefly only for the magnificent soliloquies. The opening lines of the play suggest mystery and tension. The scenes follow each other rapidly, shifting now here and now there: the battlements of the castle, the court, various rooms in the castle, a lonely plain in Denmark, a graveyard.

The major plot, of course, concerns Hamlet himself, but there are other minor plots within the play. Fortinbras, for example, that ambitious young counterpart to Hamlet, pursues his own ends throughout the play and eventually comes to have the last word. Polonius's family try to gratify their own self-interests, only to be swallowed up in the great tragedy they are sucked into. Like a helpless tree in a hurricane, these people are finally and completely destroyed. Rosencrantz and Guildenstern, too, try to watch out for themselves, only to be caught in forces too strong for them. All these minor strands are woven into the larger design that is *Hamlet*. The questions in the *Guide* will help you to follow the plot ramifications from scene to scene.

CHARACTERIZATION

In a play, as in life, you must judge people mainly by what they say and do, particularly by what they do. Sometimes, as in *Hamlet*, the playwright allows the audience a glimpse into the mind and heart of the character by the use of *asides* and *soliloquies*. An *aside* is a brief comment reflecting upon the action.

The audience hears the comment but the other actors do not. A *soliloquy* is an extended comment for the audience's benefit. During a soliloquy the character is alone on the stage as he unburdens his heart. We all engage in soliloquy, but we do not ordinarily speak our thoughts aloud. A soliloquy may be called the "spoken thoughts" of a character.

A novelist, unlike a playwright, may comment upon the action and interpret it for his readers. A novelist may tell us directly what his characters are thinking. He may explain the reactions of others to the actions of his characters. A playwright must rely upon the spoken word and the character's actions.

Why do we act as we do? Sometimes our motives are obvious and clear-cut, but sometimes they are puzzling, even to ourselves. *Hamlet*, which reflects life in all its complexities and contradictions, is a play of motivation and counter motivation. On the whole it seems obvious at first that Hamlet hesitates in his task of avenging his father's murder perhaps because he is temperamentally averse to quick action. But then on several occasions he acts quickly, heatedly, and intemperately. Critics have given dozens of explanations for Hamlet's actions, but finally every reader and spectator must decide for himself. Hamlet is as contradictory as life.

Behavior and motivation are linked closely. We understand a child's motive in seeking attention when his younger brother is temporarily in the limelight. But as the child grows older, his motivation becomes more complex, more puzzling. Some of the characters in *Hamlet* have fairly simple, clear-cut motivations, perhaps because we get to know them only superficially. But Hamlet and King Claudius, for example, are subtle and complex. Thus the actors who have played these roles have varied greatly in their interpretations. In some stage versions Claudius is a menacing bully without many redeeming traits. In other versions he is a man with many good instincts, trapped by his own passions. There are both qualities in Claudius, and the actor must decide how much weight to give to each.

As we complete each scene, we shall consider the characterizations of the persons in the scene and question their motivations when these are crucial to an understanding of the play. Because Shakespeare rarely created a flat, uninteresting character, we shall look even at the minor characters to understand Shakespeare's genius better.

STAGING AND DIRECTING

In putting on *Hamlet*, every director must make certain decisions which go beyond the text. Where should he station Claudius and Polonius during the spying scene? Should he have the courtiers laugh when Hamlet makes a bitter joke directed at Polonius or the King? What special touches should he introduce? In the movie version of *Hamlet*, for example, Laurence Olivier introduced a little dancing dog in Act II, Scene 2, to whom Hamlet spoke a line. The direction can provide many individual tricks. Though the framework of the play is fairly definite, the number of decisions up to the director is very great.

Restraint is important, too. As John Gielgud has said, "Unfortunately audiences love striking pieces of business and showmanship, and remember them long after they have forgotten the play in which they occurred." If the directorial touch is *too* dramatic and not in keeping with the spirit of the play, the effect is wasted. Still, within the possibilities of the text there are many creative touches open to directors. The questions to follow will explore the possibilities for staging and directing, and invite you to participate in the quest for good solutions to some of the problems of staging.

INTERPRETATION

"Yes, I do."

There could scarcely be a simpler statement than the preceding, and yet it has many possible oral interpretations. It may convey anger, uncertainty, determination, amusement, reassurance, indifference, sarcasm, etc. How much more difficult is it to interpret the lines in a play!

To be sure, the surrounding lines, or context, provide many clues, as does the development of the play to that point. Yet there remain many possible interpretations for the actor to choose from. The actor's conception of his role, of course, determines to a large extent how he will deliver a particular line. But even within his interpretation there are variables. He must ask himself, "Am I supposed to be angry at this point? Or feigning anger? Or indifferent? Or what?"

Part of the fun of studying the written version of a play is deciding how certain key lines should be delivered. As we study the scenes together, we shall isolate certain lines and speeches and consider how they might be presented, with you as an active participant.

LANGUAGE AND IMAGERY

"Shakespeare certainly used a lot of very famous lines!"

This comment by a student pays unconscious tribute to Shakespeare's genius, for it was Shakespeare, of course, who gave us the quotable lines. After we have studied plot and characterization, we are left with perhaps the greatest achievement of all, Shakespeare's language. His speeches dance with delight or writhe in angry torment. He can picture for us in a few words a lonely castle wall, or he can conjure up a lighthearted exchange between brother and sister.

Shakespeare's plays are written for the most part in blank verse. There are five accented syllables in each line, and the rhythm is iambic. That is, it tends to go ta **TUM** ta **TUM**. This description is an oversimplification, for Shakespeare varies the beat of his lines. Still, if you read portions of the play aloud, you can hear the subtle rhythm of blank verse give beauty and color to the words.

Shakespeare paints pictures in words. He shows us how "the morn in russet mantle clad . . . walks on the dew of yon high eastward hill." He provides a vivid and contrasting picture of man himself. He has unpleasant but vivid images of battle: England, for example, still shows the raw and red scar of the Danish arms. He pictures King Claudius as a "serpent." Line after line abounds with pictures. As we go along, we shall notice how Shakespeare's lines present vivid pictures while helping to advance the plot.

In a study of Shakespeare's skill in painting word pictures, *Shakespeare's Imagery*, Caroline Spurgeon points out that the dominant images in *Hamlet*, more than in any other play, deal with sickness, disease, corruption. Thus the feeling we get of rottenness in Denmark from the story itself is subtly reinforced.

The questions in the *Guide* will lead you to recognize and appreciate Shakespeare's genius with words.

QUESTIONS

Act I, Scene 1

This scene sets the mood of the play. We learn almost at once that something is dreadfully wrong. A ghost, in the shape of the former King Hamlet, is roaming the battlements of the castle. Denmark itself is uneasy, as a war is brewing. Young Fortinbras of Norway seems determined to win back lands lost by his father to the dead King Hamlet. The soldiers on vigil are uneasy, and they welcome the arrival of Horatio. In the course of their conversation with Horatio, they tell us a great deal about the events just preceding the opening of the play.

The great critic and poet, Samuel Taylor Coleridge, once remarked on Shakespeare's use of the first scene to advance the action. In *Macbeth* the first scene strikes the keynote of the play. In *Romeo and Juliet* the first scene relates the play to both past and future. In *The Tempest* the first scene begins the action vividly. In *Hamlet*, says Coleridge, the first scene has all these advantages at once.

One key point: to understand the role of the Ghost in *Hamlet*, we must be aware of a belief common during Shakespeare's time. Shakespearean audiences believed that devils and demons could assume a human shape in their effort to trap souls. Thus, the soldiers have no assurance that the Ghost that looks like the elder Hamlet is truly the ghost of King Hamlet.

PLOT

1. How does Shakespeare tell us that the elder Hamlet is dead? Why is it important to let us know that the elder Hamlet is dead, no longer king of Denmark?

2. Why is a strict watch being maintained on the platform before the castle? (Hint: This has nothing to do with the Ghost.)

3. Why has Marcellus invited Horatio to participate in the watch?

4. Although the Ghost of King Hamlet does not speak in this scene, we have a feeling of awe and respect toward him. Why? How does Horatio explain the Ghost's visits? Why does Horatio plan to visit young Hamlet?

5. What was the outcome of the conflict between the elder Hamlet and the elder Fortinbras? (lines 93–108) What threat does young Fortinbras now pose? (lines 108–117) How is Denmark responding to that threat? (lines 83–90)

CHARACTERIZATION

6. How does Horatio at first show himself to be skeptical about the Ghost?

7. What causes Horatio to lose his skepticism? After the entrance of the Ghost, both Marcellus and Bernardo speak twice before Horatio speaks. Why?

8. Why does Marcellus urge Horatio to speak to the Ghost?

9. When do we first hear about young Hamlet? Do not confuse young Hamlet with his father.

10. What evidence do you find in Horatio of a sense of humor, learning, daring, loyalty, and other desirable qualities?

11. The watchers respond to the Ghost with awe and respect, as well as violence. How can we explain these inconsistent responses?

STAGING AND DIRECTING

12. What clue about the setting does Shakespeare provide in each of these lines: 8, 44–47, 163, 173, 182?

13. Presenting the Ghost is a problem (e.g., lines 155–158). Shakespeare had him come up through a trap door in the stage. In modern times the Ghost may appear silently from the side of the stage. It may be seen through a semitransparent gauze with green lighting. It may be suggested by shadows and the rippling of a curtain. Shakespeare considered the Ghost an actual character, however, not a trick of Hamlet's imagination. It is usually played by a gaunt actor with a deep and resonant voice. In one production the voice of the Ghost was prerecorded. In the Lau-

rence Olivier movie version the eeriness of the Ghost's appearance was enhanced by a deeply echoing voice and swirling mists. How would *you* present the Ghost if you were the director?

INTERPRETATION

14. If *you* were acting the role of Bernardo, how would you deliver his opening line (1)? Would you try to suggest uneasiness, excitement, extreme nervousness, casualness, indifference, formality? Why?

15. Why does Francisco emphasize the word *me* in line 2? How would you deliver his line?

16. What attitude should be suggested by Francisco's speech, lines 8–9? Why is Francisco glad to be relieved at this point? Why does he twice say, "Good night"?

17. Horatio must deliver his skeptical line 37 in a manner quite different from the lines of the soldiers. How would you speak this line?

18. How does Horatio deliver line 140? Does he suggest bravado, true determination, uncertainty, bewilderment?

LANGUAGE AND IMAGERY

19. Discuss the meaning and forcefulness of each of the following images:
   a. "A mote it is to trouble the mind's eye." (line 125)
   b. "I have heard . . . To his confine." (lines 165–171)
   c. "But look, the morn . . . eastward hill." (lines 182–183)

20. Why does the tempo of the lines speed up when the Ghost appears? (line 49)

21. Shakespeare was a master of diction (choice of words). What richness of meaning does each of the following words convey?
   a. "stalks" (line 61)   d. "invulnerable" (line 161)
   b. "frown'd" (line 74)   e. "started" (line 164)
   c. "majestical" (line 159)   f. "dumb" (line 187)

Act I, Scene 2

This is a scene of great emotional intensity and dramatic importance. It introduces us to Hamlet, the King, the Queen, Polonius, and Laertes. It presents the central problem of the play, both from Hamlet's point of view and the King's. It gives Hamlet the opportunity to deliver his first soliloquy. It shows the gulf that exists between Hamlet and the pleasure-seeking court. It ties together the easygoing, frivolous society at the banquet and the uneasy, lonely battlements of the castle. While it furthers the action of the play, it keeps the audience reminded of the Ghost and his strange vigil.

PLOT

1. Several plot strands are taken up again in Scene 2: the threat from Fortinbras (lines 17–38); the death of the elder Hamlet and his replacement by Claudius (lines 1–16); the uneasiness of the Ghost. What new plot element is introduced with Laertes?
2. How have the fortunes of Claudius been affected by his brother's death?
3. How does Claudius propose to deal with young Fortinbras?
4. Claudius's eagerness to please Laertes suggests that he may be obligated in some way to Polonius. How might Polonius have helped Claudius after the elder Hamlet's death?
5. In the midst of things, the stage is cleared and Hamlet delivers his first soliloquy. (lines 131–161) The soliloquies have been interpreted as being the heart of *Hamlet*. And they have been labeled interesting bits of analysis without too much bearing on the action. At any rate, they can provide important information about the plot, as well as insights into the character's mind. What actual facts do we learn from Hamlet's first soliloquy? How does this soliloquy explain Hamlet's rude behavior to the King?
6. In the soliloquy Hamlet bitterly mentions the speed with which his mother remarried. Where in his conversation with Horatio does he show similar bitterness?
7. No time is wasted in bringing the news about the Ghost to Hamlet. Who actually breaks the news? What function do Marcellus and Bernardo serve in this scene?

8. The speeches in lines 235–260 are short. The dialogue is sharp. What is the effect of this brevity? Does this section advance the plot or merely reinforce the mood?

9. Why does Hamlet request his informants to maintain absolute secrecy about the Ghost? What does Hamlet suspect as the reason for the Ghost's appearing in armor?

10. Why is Hamlet given four lines, all by himself, at the very end of the scene? (Note the rhyme of *rise* and *eyes*. Shakespearean scenes often end in rhymed couplets.)

11. "To be sure an audience gets a point, tell them something is going to happen; then show it happening; then talk about it later." How does Shakespeare follow the last part of this suggestion in lines 203–219?

12. Hamlet's concluding speech (lines 273–276) is too short to qualify as one of the great soliloquies, but it is interesting nonetheless. It is a kind of "mini-soliloquy." Hamlet thinks aloud and expresses some of his anxieties. Notice the repetition of the word *foul*. At this point does Hamlet have any inkling of just how foul the deeds are?

CHARACTERIZATION

13. Claudius's opening speech is a kind of inaugural address. He has the problems of justifying his marriage so soon after the death of the elder Hamlet, of winning the support of the court, and of showing himself to be a strong leader. In his attack on these problems as well as in his later remarks to Hamlet, what use does Claudius make of (a) "practical" logic? (b) Flattery? (c) Decisive action?

14. Critics have often pointed out that, except for Hamlet and later Horatio, the King seems to be popular with the members of the court. What evidences do we find that the court fully accepts Claudius as king?

15. It is typical of Hamlet's character that he uses irony, wit, and humor to deal with hateful situations. Give at least three examples from Scene II of this characteristic of Hamlet.

16. Hamlet has a brilliant mind and he is a master of words. How does he show this mastery in (a) his answer to his mother (lines 78–88)? (b) His soliloquy (lines 131–161)?

17. What do we learn from Hamlet's soliloquy (lines 131–161) about his feelings toward his father? His mother? His uncle?

18. What are Gertrude's motives in lines 69–74 and 120–121? Is she more concerned for Claudius or for Hamlet? Why?

19. Claudius allows Laertes to leave the court, but he refuses to allow Hamlet to go. What motive can you suggest for this refusal?

20. In this scene the King does most of the talking. The Queen says very little. What does that possibly suggest about the relationship of the King and the Queen? Which person seems the dominant one?

21. What characteristic of Polonius is illustrated by his answer to Claudius's question? (lines 59–62).

22. Explain Hamlet's absentmindedness in line 164, when he fails to recognize his friend Horatio.

23. Note the sharp contrast between Hamlet's first words to Claudius (lines 66, 68) and his greeting of Horatio (lines 163–164 and following). What further evidences does this scene provide of genuine friendship between Hamlet and Horatio?

24. This is the second time we meet Horatio. Does his character in this scene seem consistent with his earlier characterization?

25. Notice that again, in talking of the Ghost, Horatio says not "your father," but "a figure like your father." In line 209 he uses the pronoun *he* but in line 222 Hamlet uses the pronoun *it*. What does that suggest about Hamlet's uncertainty about the Ghost? This uncertainty is an important element right up to the play scene.

STAGING AND DIRECTING

26. How does the setting of Scene 2 contrast with that of Scene 1, which was played in gloom? What is the dramatic effect of such contrast?

27. The courtiers provide important background for the King throughout. Since the King is a person of some dread, George Bernard Shaw suggests that they should listen attentively while the King is speaking. In some productions they chatter and are inattentive. John Gielgud suggests that they should include mostly people of the age of Claudius and Gertrude. In many productions they are young. As you read the play, try to visualize these important background players. What should they be doing? How should they respond?

INTERPRETATION

28. Claudius addresses Hamlet a number of times in the scene, but Hamlet answers Claudius directly only once. (line 68) How does Hamlet clearly snub the King?

29. What point is made if Hamlet emphasizes the word *you* in line 122?

30. The King is not insensitive and is probably aware of Hamlet's snubbing; yet he chooses to disregard it. Why? If you were playing the King, how would you deliver line 123? After all, Hamlet has just snubbed the King by agreeing to obey the *Queen*.

31. Another climactic line is 195. Should Hamlet express amazement, intense curiosity, fright?

32. If you were delivering the soliloquy (lines 131–161), what would your dominant emotion be? John Gielgud considers this the most exciting of the soliloquies because it provides essential material for the entire plot and is dramatically a powerhouse.

33. How do lines 141–144 require a different tone from those immediately preceding and following? Remember that at this moment Hamlet is thinking of his father, whom he loved dearly.

34. How would you read "She married," in line 158?

35. In line 188 Hamlet says, "Methinks I see my father." How would you deliver Horatio's reply, "O where, my lord?" Why might Horatio turn quickly around in fright as he delivers the line?

36. The reading of line 192 has sometimes been debated. How would you interpret it? Would you emphasize *man*?

37. Why did Shakespeare give line 221 to Marcellus instead of Horatio? Why include Marcellus at all? Would you have Marcellus deliver his line differently from the way Horatio speaks?

38. In line 253 the two soldiers cry out, "Longer, longer," after Horatio has guessed at the length of the Ghost's visit. How would you deliver this line? How does it add a note of realism to this unusual scene?

LANGUAGE AND IMAGERY

39. Claudius balances each reference to joy over his marriage to Gertrude with an expression of grief at the death of her first husband, e.g., "defeated joy."
   a. Find three similar expressions in Claudius's opening speech.
   b. What is Claudius's purpose in using such language?

40. The image of sun and shadow, light and dark is strong in the first exchange between Hamlet and Claudius and Gertrude. (lines 67–68, 69, and 79–80) How does this contrast in images suggest a contrast in personalities?

41. In lines 103–104, Claudius suggests that excessive grief is a fault in three different ways. What are they?

42. What do the following suggest?
   a. "Green" (line 2)
   b. "Weary, stale, flat, and unprofitable" (line 135)
   c. "Hyperion to a satyr" (line 142)

43. Hamlet compares the world to an "unweeded garden." (lines 137–139) In what way, according to Hamlet, are they similar?

44. Why do you agree or disagree with Hamlet's oft-quoted remark, "Frailty, thy name is woman"? (line 148)

Act I, Scene 3

This scene provides a change of pace in the headlong action involving the Ghost. While the audience is eagerly awaiting the confrontation of Hamlet and the Ghost, Shakespeare makes everyone wait while he leisurely shows us the household of

Polonius. There is an air of light and brightness that provides an interlude between the gloom of Scene 1 and the shadowy actions of Scene 4. It has none of the bitterness of Scene 2.

Even though this scene provides a dramatic change, it does more. It shows us Laertes leaving, after having secured permission in Scene 2. It tells us something about Hamlet's presumed love for Ophelia. In Polonius's action forbidding further contact between Ophelia and Hamlet, we have a definite element in the development of the plot. It also reveals some of the weaknesses of Polonius's family.

PLOT

1. What advice does Laertes give Ophelia about Hamlet? Why does he tell her not to hope for Hamlet's love?

2. What advice does Polonius give Ophelia?

3. Why are lines 88–89 important to the plot? Note that Polonius is listening intently.

4. What proof is there that Hamlet has loved Ophelia?

5. In view of Hamlet's state of mind as it has resulted from his mother's marriage and Claudius's kingship, how is Ophelia's obedience to her father's command likely to affect him?

CHARACTERIZATION

6. A major purpose of this scene is to introduce Ophelia. How do lines 2–13 and 48–55 clearly show that there is a warm relationship between Laertes and Ophelia?

7. As "big brother," Laertes is giving "little sister" the benefit of his superior wisdom. How does Ophelia turn the tables in lines 49–54?

8. How does Ophelia show herself a dutiful daughter in line 141? Should she have spoken up and protested against her father's ruling? What does her behavior in this instance tell us about her character?

9. How does Shakespeare show us that Polonius likes to hear himself talk? What do you learn about the extent to which Polonius practices what he preaches?

10. What is Ophelia's feeling toward Hamlet?

11. Does Polonius seem more concerned about Ophelia's welfare or about his own position at court? See especially line 114.

12. Is the characterization of Polonius here consistent with the brief characterization we had of him in Scene 2?

13. Laertes has been called a "young Polonius." Is there any justification in this scene for such a label?

STAGING AND DIRECTING

14. If you were the stage director, would you choose bright lighting for this scene, or would you keep the lighting subdued? Give reasons for your plan.

15. Some directors have indicated a portion of a ship visible through a window in the room. What is the dramatic purpose of such an item? What justification can we find in the lines themselves for such a device?

INTERPRETATION

16. In line 11, "No more but so?" Ophelia gives us some indication of her personality. This can be read to suggest a sly sense of humor, a complete indifference to what Laertes is saying, a very serious reaction to a very serious suggestion, or an argumentative disagreement with his point of view. Which would you favor?

17. In lines 55–56 Laertes also can suggest many things by the way he delivers his lines. He may suddenly realize he has been long-winded and apologetically reply to Ophelia. He may retain the high moralistic tone that he maintained in the long speech just preceding. He may speak the lines hurriedly, hoping to avoid a lengthy lecture from his father. He may suggest sarcasm, humor, openness. What would you choose?

18. Why does Ophelia emphasize *me* in line 51?

19. Polonius's famous speech, lines 62–85, has been interpreted in many ways — for example, as the chatter of a talkative old man or as the weighty advice of a sage old counselor. Much depends upon how the lines are delivered. How would you read the portion beginning "to thine own self be true"?

20. Laertes' farewell, with his mention of remembering "what I have said to you," (lines 88–89) is important. Polonius must pick up the clue and pursue it, so that he can tell Ophelia not to see Hamlet any longer. How would you deliver this line so that Polonius can overhear it?

21. Some actors have delivered the last farewell of Laertes (line 92) with obvious impatience. What does such an interpretation add to the scene?

22. Some actors who play Polonius emphasize the words *my* and *your* in line 102. Read the line with this interpretation. Does it seem like a good interpretation? Why?

23. In line 106 Polonius shows very pointedly what his opinion of Ophelia is. How would you deliver this line? How would you suggest sarcasm in line 108?

24. Read lines 115–116, emphasizing *honorable*. What is the reason for this reading?

25. In lines 118–119 Ophelia hopes to sway Polonius to her point of view toward Hamlet. How should these lines be delivered?

LANGUAGE AND IMAGERY

26. "The primrose path" (line 53) has passed over into the language and is defined in the dictionary as "the path of ease and pleasure." How does the dictionary definition fit the context here?

27. Polonius says, "The wind sits in the shoulder of your sail." (line 60) What picture does the word *shoulder* suggest to you?

28. In his famous advice to Laertes, Polonius uses many figures of speech — for example, "grapple them to thy soul with hoops of steel"; "loan oft loses both itself and friend"; "borrowing dulls the edge of husbandry (thrift)." Choose one of these to explain.

29. The color green was used in line 2 of Scene 2. Here again, in line 106, it is used to suggest freshness, but here the element of inexperience is added. Is the connotation intended to be favorable here?

Act I, Scene 4

Scene 4 takes us back to the battlements of the castle. As the scene opens, Hamlet and his uneasy companions are pacing the parapets. Then we are allowed to follow the main thread of action as the Ghost reappears. But since the information the Ghost imparts must be given to Hamlet alone, Hamlet is separated from his comrades in following the Ghost offstage.

The scene is important because it marks the first confrontation between the Ghost and Hamlet. The play has been leading up to this crucial event. Though it is a short scene, it is intensely dramatic.

PLOT

1. Who first sees the Ghost? Who then speaks to it at length?

2. Why does Shakespeare have Horatio and Marcellus try to restrain Hamlet from going with the Ghost?

3. This scene prepares the audience for the dramatic revelations to be made by the Ghost. Why does Shakespeare delay the revelations still further at this point?

CHARACTERIZATION

4. The Ghost must remain a figure of dignity and dread. How does Marcellus emphasize the dignity of this mysterious figure in line 64?

5. Hamlet has been called a figure of hesitation and inaction. How do lines 90–95 disprove this picture and thus show that he can never be summed up in a few simple words?

6. Hamlet disapproves of the King and his pleasure-seeking court. How do lines 16–40 reinforce this disapproval?

7. How does Horatio continue to show his unselfish concern for Hamlet?

8. Note that Marcellus again appears. Although it is a minor role, Marcellus is a person of some substance and character. How does he show an independence and dignity in this scene?

9. Why does the Ghost wish to speak to Hamlet alone?

10. Hamlet says, "I do not set my life at a pin's fee." (line 71) What does that line tell us of Hamlet's mood as reflected here and in Scene 2?

STAGING AND DIRECTING

11. Shakespeare always has a feeling for human emotions and human reactions. The opening dialogue of the scene is very natural. It doesn't advance the plot, but it helps set the mood. How does the atmosphere remind us of Scene 1?

12. Why must the lighting of this scene be somber? What is the mood of the scene? How do the opening lines set the stage, even without scenery? (Note that the uncertainty about time adds to the tension.)

INTERPRETATION

13. Lines 47–48 are often debated. There are at least two possible readings. Different editors of the play punctuate the play differently to suggest the two readings. In one reading, "Hamlet, King, father" are grouped together; then "royal Dane" goes with "O, answer me!" In the second reading, the four labels are grouped together: "Hamlet, King, father, royal Dane." The first possibility has the word "father" as the climax. The second has "royal Dane" as the climax. Read the lines aloud both ways. Which do you prefer? Why?

14. Line 60 is interesting to play with. Try emphasizing *should*; then emphasize *do*. What difference is there?

15. The actor who plays Horatio sometimes emphasizes the second *no* in line 67. What effect does this emphasis have?

16. Some Hamlets emphasize *thee* in line 86. Try it. What additional meaning does this reading suggest?

LANGUAGE AND IMAGERY

17. The uncertainty about time adds to tension. Hamlet's speech when the Ghost appears is filled with excitement, tension, dread, and pure poetry. Even though Hamlet fears this may be a devil, he says that he will address the Ghost. He says, "I'll call thee Hamlet." But in line 68, he says he will follow *it* not *him*. What does this tell us about the degree of certainty of Hamlet's feeling toward the Ghost?

18. Note that the graveyard images in lines 50–57, though awesome, are yet effective, even beautiful in their way. What does he compare the grave with?

19. Explain the imagery used by Horatio (lines 75–84) as he tries to warn Hamlet not to meddle with the Ghost.

20. How does Hamlet display his wry sense of humor in line 94?

21. Line 99, "Something is rotten in the state of Denmark," is often quoted, and misquoted. What evidences have we already had in the play that all is not well in Denmark? What universal meaning may the line have?

Act I, Scene 5

In a sense, this scene is merely a continuation of the previous scene. But this scene realizes what Scene 4 merely looks toward: the revelation by the Ghost of the reasons for his walking the battlements. Scene 5, by revealing to Hamlet (and the audience) the murder of Hamlet's father by Claudius, sets in motion the plot elements that do not stop until the end of the play. It is thus a key scene in the play.

In this scene Hamlet must determine his future strategy. By swearing Marcellus and Horatio to silence, Hamlet suggests that he is buying time before deciding just what steps to take.

The Ghost's description of his torments suggests that he is in Purgatory, a place of suffering necessary because of his unsanctified death. Claudius's murder of King Hamlet has doomed Hamlet "to walk the night" until his soul is cleansed. Thus Claudius has not only cruelly treated King Hamlet in his earthly life; he has given him over to torment in the life after death.

Critics have pointed out a number of different attitudes toward the Ghost. Marcellus accepted the Ghost without question. Horatio at first doubted its existence. Hamlet thought it might be a demon from Hell to tempt him to sin. The Ghost himself, however, suggests that he is a spirit assigned to Purgatory for a while. Hamlet's uncertainty about the nature of the Ghost is important to the plot.

PLOT

1. What important information does this scene provide about the crime, the way in which the crime was committed, the murderer, and the results of that crime?

2. What terrible responsibility does the Ghost lay upon Hamlet?

3. Since the crime was perpetrated in secret, which three characters at this point are the only ones who know about it? Notice that the Ghost absolves Gertrude of any part in the murder.

4. Why does Hamlet swear Horatio and Marcellus to secrecy? Why doesn't he tell the two men what the Ghost has told him? (He seems about to tell them in lines 127–133.)

5. In line 191 Hamlet says that he may "put an antic disposition on." In other words, he may begin to act strangely. This important statement prepares the audience for Hamlet's strange behavior later on. What does he warn Horatio and Marcellus not to do?

6. Since Hamlet is so upset after his encounter with the Ghost, how might Marcellus and Bernardo interpret the Ghost — as a good or evil influence on Hamlet?

7. Lines 98–118 constitute the second soliloquy of Hamlet. How does Hamlet show that he is emotionally overwrought by the new responsibilities placed upon him?

8. In his soliloquy Hamlet *first* mentions his mother ("pernicious woman") and *then* Claudius ("villain, smiling, damned villain"). How do these references give us insight into Hamlet's two greatest emotional problems?

9. Lines 46–47 ("O my prophetic soul! My uncle!") have been debated often. One school of critics suggests that Hamlet has suspected all along that his uncle was guilty of the murder. Another school suggests that the line merely provides a more reasonable basis for Hamlet's intense hatred of Claudius, a hatred that up to now has been based only on the too-hasty marriage. Which interpretation do you think more likely?

10. Hamlet tells the Ghost to inform him so that he "May sweep to my revenge." (line 35) Why is that revenge likely to be difficult? (Hamlet takes the rest of the play to reach that goal.)

11. In line 152 Hamlet says, "It is an honest ghost, that let me tell you." What does Hamlet mean by this line? Is he trying to convince himself and remove lingering doubts? (Later Hamlet *still* wishes to make sure by arranging the play scene!)

12. In one view of the play the main problem of Hamlet is that he is put into a bind. No matter which way he turns, the knots tighten. He must avenge his father's death, but he must make the death of Claudius justice, not murder. However, the world will consider it murder unless people know that Claudius murdered the elder Hamlet. But how can Hamlet make this known? It all hangs upon the word of a ghost — and the Ghost may be a devil. Supernatural agencies move Hamlet to action and perhaps to sin, but these same agencies reveal to him the terrors of punishment in the afterlife. No wonder Hamlet is upset! How do lines 209–210 suggest this terrible dilemma?

CHARACTERIZATION

13. This is the Ghost's great scene. From his words we can deduce the kind of person King Hamlet was in life. What evidences do we find in his speech of his basic courage, his bitterness toward Claudius, his loving tenderness toward Gertrude, his keen sense of justice?

14. What evidences do we find in this scene of Hamlet's great love for his father?

15. What picture do we get of Claudius in the Ghost's description of him? How does this picture differ from the Claudius we have met in Scene 2?

16. What picture do we get of Gertrude? How does this picture differ from the Gertrude we have met in Scene 2?

17. How does Hamlet show his emotional upset after Horatio and Marcellus rejoin him?

18. How do Marcellus and Horatio indicate by their words that they are fond of Hamlet?

19. In the midst of this tragedy Shakespeare is capable of many little human touches, as in lines 125–138. Horatio and Marcellus are eager to know what the Ghost has said, and they hasten to assure Hamlet that they won't breathe a word. What abrupt change of thought does Hamlet seem to have after beginning his remark in line 135? What do you suppose he had originally meant to say? How does this little touch add to the audience's satisfaction?

STAGING AND DIRECTING

20. When Hamlet says, "My tables — meet it is I set it down" (line 113), some productions actually have Hamlet take out a writing pad and jot down something on it. Other productions omit this business and make the reference to tables a more figurative one, for example, by pointing to the head. How would you solve this problem?

21. Marcellus and Horatio seem to come rushing onto the scene as though they have been hastening to find Hamlet. How does the setting help to establish their sense of urgency?

22. In Shakespearean times the Ghost came up through a trap-door in the stage floor and descended through it. Thus his voice seems to be coming up through the floor as he cries out, "Swear!" (The stage directions actually say "Beneath.") Why would that source of the Ghost's voice add a sense of dread for the Shakespearean audience?

INTERPRETATION

23. In line 13 the Ghost says, "I am thy father's spirit." How would you read this line? Perhaps *am* should be emphasized. What does this emphasis accomplish?

24. What feeling does Hamlet suggest in the opening line of this scene? How does the line prepare for the emotional revelations in the following lines?

25. "Murder!" in line 30 includes an exclamation point. It may suggest surprise, horror, shock, incredulousness, bitterness, dismay, or other emotions. Which emotion or combination of emotions would you wish to suggest by your interpretation?

26. In lines 101 and 103 Hamlet repeats the phrase "Remember thee!" What differences can you suggest in the reading of the two instances of this phrase?

27. How would you read Horatio's "What news, my lord?" (line 126)

28. There is a reminder of the basic conflict in the play in these two lines, "that I may sweep to my revenge," and "O cursed spite, that ever I was born to set it right." How do these two lines suggest the basic problem of *Hamlet* the play and Hamlet the man?

LANGUAGE AND IMAGERY

29. The Ghost presents a terrifying picture of his position in Purgatory, the place where sinners are cleansed. His use of the word *purg'd* provides a clue. Yet the horror is suggested, never directly detailed. What effect might there be on Hamlet if the Ghost were able to tell about his "prison-house"? Why is the suggestion more terrifying than an exact description?

30. Shakespeare is a master of instant contrasts. In the midst of the Ghost's bitter attacks on Claudius, there is a pause and a change of pace as the Ghost says, "But, soft! methinks I scent the morning air." What is the dramatic effect of this quiet interlude?

31. "Leave her to heaven" is a phrase from *Hamlet* that also served as the title of a book. As you go along, find other phrases that have passed into the language or have been used as book titles. Can you suggest from the play this far a phrase that might serve as a good book title?

32. Notice that in line 185 Hamlet says, "There are more things in heaven and earth, Horatio, than are dreamt of in your philosophy." Why is the mention of *heaven* particularly appropriate at this point?

Act II, Scene 1

This scene has two parts. The first of these, in which Polonius sends his servant Reynaldo off to spy on his son Laertes, is often reduced or cut altogether in acting versions. The second portion is crucial to the play, for in it Ophelia tells us of Hamlet's changed behavior. Of course, the audience knows more than Ophelia and has some idea of the reason for Hamlet's "new look." But Ophelia and Polonius completely misinterpret the situation and, in doing so, advance the plot.

The Reynaldo portion of this scene has little dramatic value, except to remind us that Laertes is off in Paris having a good time. We have to remember Laertes, since he'll be playing a crucial part later. But there is another value to this segment: it is funny. It shows us Polonius as a living embodiment of the "generation gap," and it adds a needed lighter touch after the intensely dramatic moments of the preceding scene. Life is alternately bright and dark, up and down, sad and humorous. Shakespeare, with his unerring instinct for depicting life, never hesitated to insert comedy into the midst of tragedy.

PLOT

1. In the preceding scene Hamlet has told Horatio (and the audience) that he may "put an antic disposition on." What news does Ophelia give us about Hamlet's actions and appearance? What is the dramatic value of having the telling and the doing come so close together? In your opinion what is the true explanation of Hamlet's behavior?

2. How does Polonius react to the news of Hamlet's strange actions?

3. Polonius wastes no time in going to the King with the news about Hamlet. Why will the King be eager to get such news?

4. What evidence is there that Hamlet truly loved Ophelia?

CHARACTERIZATION

5. Polonius tends to talk too much. This trait becomes more and more apparent as the play progresses. How does this scene further illuminate the character of Polonius?

6. Reynaldo is the perfect servant, but we suspect his evaluation of Polonius is not unlike ours. Is there any clue to his true feelings toward Polonius?

7. What trait of Polonius is revealed by his plans to spy on his son? What does this information tell us about both Polonius and Laertes?

8. In his spying, Polonius wants Reynaldo to say that Laertes is wild and unreliable. What is Polonius's motive? How does Reynaldo start to object?

9. In lines 95–96 Ophelia shows her complete misjudgment of Hamlet's change in behavior. What does this understandable error tell us about Ophelia?

10. How does Ophelia tell us, unknowingly, that she may have failed Hamlet when he needed her?

11. Polonius wants to tell the King immediately that Hamlet has been made mad by Ophelia's rejection. What is Polonius's relationship to the King?

12. How does Polonius show himself to be a poor judge of Hamlet?

13. Ophelia has done exactly what her father told her to do. What does this admission tell us about Ophelia and Polonius?

14. In this scene Hamlet, known to the audience as sensible and idealistic, is reported to be playing a role opposed to his temperament. The King, known to the audience as a murderer, has, in Act I, Scene 2, assumed the role of noble, generous, kindhearted monarch. How does this double contrast sharpen the characterizations of both Hamlet and Claudius?

STAGING AND DIRECTING

15. Act 1, Scene 3 and this scene merely say, "A room in Polonius's house." If you were staging this, would you use the same set for both scenes? Why or why not?

16. The movies are able to show scenes which are described in *Hamlet* not acted out on stage. In a movie version, as Ophelia delivers lines 86–93, 98–111, Hamlet can be pictured going through these motions. Would this device add to the production or detract from it?

INTERPRETATION

17. The actor who plays Reynaldo has only a small part, but in this scene he has a chance to play it well. Some interpretations of this scene have Reynaldo, obviously bored and eager to get on his way, backing toward the door. Then as he reaches the door (line 81), he quickly says, "Well, my lord!" and disappears. Polonius has to call after him, "Farewell!" How might such an interpretation sharpen the characterization of Polonius?

18. Reynaldo is studiously polite; Polonius is long-winded. The two characterizations are particularly well drawn in lines 54–59. How would you read these lines?

19. Polonius's major error is revealed in line 94, "Mad for thy love?" How would you read this line and Ophelia's reply?

LANGUAGE AND IMAGERY

20. Polonius's directions to Reynaldo are less famous and less often quoted than his advice to Laertes (Act 1, Scene 3). Yet they do contain a famous statement: "With assays of bias, by indirections find directions out." In other words, more can be learned by being devious and underhanded than by being straightforward and honest. Do you agree with Polonius? Can you give examples to illustrate his point? How does his order further reveal Polonius's character to us?

21. Ophelia's picture of Hamlet in his supposed madness is vivid. Point out evidences, as Ophelia sees them, of Hamlet's breakdown.

Act II, Scene 2

This is a long and very important scene. It is by far the longest scene in the play. It might be divided into several sections: the arrival of Rosencrantz and Guildenstern; the episode with the ambassadors to Norway; Polonius's interpretation of Hamlet's madness; the meeting of Hamlet and his two schoolfellows; the arrival of the players. Each section advances the plot. Each section develops key characterizations.

The scene also provides a setting for what may be the most dramatic of Hamlet's soliloquies. It gives us insight into Hamlet's mind to a far greater degree than before. It sets the stage for the important play scene that follows. In the chess game between Hamlet and Claudius, important moves and countermoves are made in this scene. We get the feeling that Claudius is no fool. He has been extremely wary of this potentially dangerous young man.

As you study the play, however, keep in mind that the division of the play into acts and scenes is not Shakespeare's work but the work of later editors. Actors and directors of Shakespeare's time were more interested in keeping the play moving than in setting up acts and scenes as such.

PLOT

1. How is the problem of young Fortinbras solved? What concession has Norway made to quiet the fiery youth? (This mention of Fortinbras helps prepare the audience for his appearance at the end of the play. Fortinbras actually appears in only two scenes.)

2. What explanation does Polonius give for Hamlet's apparent insanity? Why would the King prefer this explanation to be true? (The King's eagerness to learn the cause of Hamlet's odd behavior is revealed in line 53: "O! speak of that; that do I long to hear." Polonius has to remind Claudius to see the ambassadors first.)

3. Why has the King summoned Rosencrantz and Guildenstern? Why does he think they may be able to help him?

4. What plan does Polonius concoct to prove that Hamlet is mad for love of Ophelia? (The critic John Dover Wilson argues that Hamlet overhears the plot and is seen by the audience in the background. Other critics disagree strongly and say there is nothing in the play to warrant this interpretation.)

5. Why are Rosencrantz and Guildenstern so reluctant to tell Hamlet the real reason for their presence at the court?

6. Who first tells us that the players are coming? Who says that they have actually arrived? How does Hamlet plan to use the players for his own purposes?

7. At times Hamlet seems recklessly compelled to give himself away. What information does Hamlet actually give Rosencrantz and Guildenstern in lines 382–386? What might a clever observer read into this admission?

8. In Act I, Scene 5, Hamlet said, "It is an honest ghost." Yet in lines 607–608 he says, "The spirit that I have seen may be the devil." What has evidently happened as Hamlet has thought about the strange events? How does line 611 show one of Hamlet's fears about possible actions?

9. In this scene how does Hamlet further baffle Polonius?

10. Each character forms his own opinion about the source of Hamlet's madness. Polonius thinks it is rejected love. Gertrude thinks it is her too-hasty marriage after the death of King Hamlet. Rosencrantz and Guildenstern wonder whether it is frustrated ambition. (lines 262–263) Only the King withholds judgment. He is no fool. He is a worthy opponent for Hamlet. Why is it important dramatically to have Claudius and Hamlet fairly evenly matched?

CHARACTERIZATION

11. Rosencrantz and Guildenstern appear on the scene, summoned by the King. Their motives have been the subject of debate. Their lives have been the subject of a fascinating play, *Rosencrantz and Guildenstern Are Dead*. Are they scheming spies without conscience or scruples, as critics suggest? Or are they poor dupes of circumstance, buffeted back and forth without a clear knowledge of where they are and what they are doing? From this first scene in which they appear, what is your opinion of them?

12. How does the King show his subtlety and cleverness as he explains to Rosencrantz and Guildenstern why they were called for?

13. What evidence is there that Hamlet once thought highly of Rosencrantz and Guildenstern?

14. What evidence do we have that the Queen feels a bit guilty at her hasty marriage? (The Queen says very little in this scene, but we learn about her from the few things she does say and from the attitude of Claudius toward her. It seems clear that she knows nothing of King Hamlet's murder.)

15. How does Hamlet's first reaction to the meeting with Rosencrantz and Guildenstern contrast with his behavior after he learns they are acting as agents for the King?

16. Why does Hamlet blame himself in his great soliloquy, beginning with line 555? Why does he contrast himself with the player? What indications are there that Hamlet is very much upset at this time?

17. Some critics feel that Hamlet is closest to insanity in lines 577–582, but the problem is difficult to pin down. After all, Hamlet has told us he will act strangely. There are relative degrees of disturbance and upset. Hamlet has had much provocation and has been upset by events. Perhaps we should all break out in an emotional outburst like this with similar provocation. Why is it impossible to answer finally the questions, "In his unusual behavior how much is Hamlet pretending? How much is his behavior a reflection of his actual feelings?"

18. Hamlet, probably like Shakespeare, loved acting. In his welcome to the players he actually can't wait to act out some lines himself. Why is his ability to act, to play a role, important in the development of the plot of *Hamlet*?

19. Once again (lines 587–588) Hamlet uses the word *villain* in referring to his uncle. If Hamlet is still uncertain about his uncle's guilt in the murder of Hamlet's father, why does he use such violent language in talking about him? (Note that Hamlet has called himself *villain* in line 578).

20. Claudius is very careful in dealing with Hamlet. Hamlet, however, is not always as careful in his statements to Claudius. Does Hamlet's comment about Denmark as a prison (lines 252, 254) and about Claudius (line 383) show a certain recklessness? What is his motive in being so open and direct?

STAGING AND DIRECTING

21. How would you stage the long soliloquy, lines 555–613? How could you dramatize, by set and lighting, the intensity and the loneliness of the scene?

22. Reference to the "late innovation," line 342, is used by some critics to date the play. The late innovation, or recent change, refers to the formation of companies of child actors to present plays in London. Why would Shakespeare be so violently opposed to this kind of competition?

INTERPRETATION

23. The soliloquy (lines 555–613), the third in the play, has been delivered by actors with every imaginable kind of interpretation. A comparison of different recordings by different actors reveals the widest variation. If you were delivering the soliloquy, to what lines would you give most emphasis? Which lines would you understate? How would you conclude the soliloquy? Would you try to suggest uncertainty, firmness, determination, anger, anxiety, nervousness, dread? (George Bernard Shaw called *this* the "great soliloquy," not the "to be" soliloquy. The modern critic Norman N. Holland agrees with him.)

24. Most interpretations of the soliloquy break the mood sharply after line 589. The speech rises to a dramatic crescendo. Then, as if it can go no higher, it pauses and falls. Line 590 seems like a calm reflection after the bitter cry of "O, vengeance!"

Interpretations of this soliloquy vary greatly. They provide a clue to the author's understanding of the character of Hamlet. John Barrymore made this an extremely emotional scene. Nicoll Williamson, on the other hand, played it in a much more restrained fashion.

How would recordings of the same speech by different actors help you to deepen your own understanding of the play?

25. Audiences have always had difficulty trying to keep Rosencrantz and Guildenstern straight. Some stage versions of the play show the King to be as confused as the audience! In line 35 the King greets the pair. In the next line the Queen also greets them, but she reverses the order, perhaps to straighten them out in the King's mind. If you wanted to suggest a touch of humor to show the King confused about which is which, how would you read line 36? (Some critics have suggested that the Queen is merely emphasizing the equality of Rosencrantz and Guildenstern in reversing the names.)

26. How would you read line 53 to suggest the King's eagerness on the topic of Hamlet's eccentric behavior?

27. The Queen is less patient with Polonius's long-windedness than the King. How would you read line 102 to suggest irritation at Polonius's failure to get to the point?

28. Line 121 is an interesting line to play with. Is the Queen suggesting disbelief, hope, irritation? Consider how you would emphasize, or fail to emphasize, words like *this*, *Hamlet*, and *her*.

29. There is a touch of humor in the King's retort to Polonius. (line 165) How would you read this to bring out the sly fun in the remark?

30. Line 207 is typical of Hamlet's responses. When he dislikes a character, his response shows a deliberate misinterpretation of the character's words. The three people he particularly despises as shown in this way are Claudius, Polonius, and — later — Osric. How does line 219 show this same contempt?

31. Actors have wrestled with line 205: "Words, words, words." Do you think these separate words should be repeated with about the same emphasis, or should they be read differently? Should there be a pause somewhere?

32. In some productions of *Hamlet* lines 319–321 are said bitterly. How would you read these lines?

33. Guildenstern's admission to Hamlet, line 302, has had varied interpretations. First read the line to emphasize *were*. Then read "We were sent for" without particular emphasis on any word. What difference in interpretation is suggested by these two readings?

34. Lines 393–395 show a clear break after "Mark it." Hamlet has been talking privately with the players. Then as Polonius enters, he says aloud, "You say right, sir," and the rest. This latter speech is merely to mislead Polonius. How would you read the three lines to suggest this break?

35. In the Paul Scofield *Hamlet* presented by the Shakespeare Recording Society, lines 534–538 are presented lightly. The actors laugh as Hamlet asks, "Who shall 'scape whipping?" Richard Burton's interpretation, by contrast, is bitter and sharp. There is no laughter. If possible, listen to these contrasting recordings. Note how much leeway an actor has in interpreting a play. Which interpretation do you prefer here?

36. Hamlet is a master of irony. Lines 548–549 are said with sarcasm. How would you read them?

LANGUAGE AND IMAGERY

37. About a hundred years ago, H. H. Furness, a Shakespearean scholar, gathered together the critical commentary about the various lines in Shakespearean plays. Since there are variations in the lines and since there is no absolutely certain version of *Hamlet*, scholars have debated which lines are correct. In line 57, for example, we are not sure whether Claudius says, "My dear Gertrude" or "My sweet Queen." In the Furness study, called the *Variorum Edition*, the editor quotes one critic as suggesting that "My dear Gertrude" means the honeymoon is over. "My sweet Queen," to this critic, seemed more endearing. What do you think? Which version do you prefer?

38. Shakespeare enjoyed irony at times. He gives one of the most famous and, in this setting, ironic lines to Polonius (line 96): "Since brevity is the soul of wit . . . I will be brief." Why is this line ironic as spoken by Polonius?

39. Shakespeare also enjoyed punning. In line 206 he has Polonius ask, "What is the matter?" (What are you reading?) Hamlet intentionally misunderstands and replies, "Between who?" (What is Hamlet's purpose in deliberately misunderstanding Polonius?)

40. Polonius, often given quotable lines, is also given the famous, "Though this be madness, yet there is method in 't." (line 217) Find other famous Polonius lines earlier in the play.

41. The expression "caviar to the general" (line 442–443) has passed into the language. What does it mean? (Hint: "General" means the majority of people, not the military rank.)

42. Shakespeare uses prose, instead of poetry, for many of the speeches in this scene — for example, the reentrance of Rosencrantz and Guildenstern. Some critics have suggested that the prose adds variety and changes the tempo. Do you prefer the poetry or the prose?

43. Hamlet's poetic description of earth and man (lines 309–321) is in prose. Yet it is one of the most poetic descriptions in the play. What are the two deeply felt views of life and the world given here? Select one especially strong and vivid image representing each view.

Act III, Scene 1

This scene contains the most famous of the Hamlet soliloquies: "To be or not to be." Dramatically, however, the soliloquy is overshadowed by the King's awareness, at last, that Hamlet's supposed madness may be a danger to the crown. Polonius and Ophelia share the disillusionment, but for different reasons.

PLOT

1. What information does the King seek as he questions Rosencrantz and Guildenstern? What information can they give him?

2. What does Claudius tell Gertrude about his plan for spying on Hamlet?

3. Up to this point Claudius has entertained the possibility that Hamlet's madness may be traced to rejected love, but he has not embraced this idea with any assurance. How does his realization of his danger change the direction of the plot?

4. How does the Queen's question in lines 16–17 prepare us again for the play scene?

5. Hamlet's cold rejection of Ophelia, together with his treatment of her in the next scene, prepares the way for her tragedy later. She influences the plot in two ways: to provide some cover at first for Hamlet's supposed lunacy; and to goad Laertes to revenge later. Note that Ophelia, like Rosencrantz and Guildenstern, is on the fringes of the action and suffers the consequences of being involved in matters too complex and too dangerous for her. What is your attitude toward this unfortunate girl?

6. There are two important plot outcomes of this scene. Claudius makes an important decision regarding Hamlet, and Polonius has a plan for a meeting involving Hamlet. What are these two plans?

7. Hamlet recklessly calls out those qualities that are most menacing to the King: pride, revenge, ambition. (lines 134–135) Why does he mention these qualities at this point?

CHARACTERIZATION

8. Rosencrantz and Guildenstern are differentiated a bit in lines 5–10. What two slightly different reports do they give?

9. Why does the King use the words "turbulent and dangerous lunacy" (line 4) in talking to Rosencrantz and Guildenstern about Hamlet? Why is the King uneasy? Why is he eager to find the cause?

10. It is interesting that the Queen says, in line 42, "I shall obey you." Throughout the play she does indeed obey Claudius, except for a fatal disobedience in the last scene. Who else, thus far, has shown a blind obedience to the commands of another?

11. After the scene with Ophelia, Claudius says bitterly, "Love! his affections do not that way tend," (line 174) and then shows that he, Claudius, is uneasy. How does he show himself capable of acting quickly to contain the possible danger?

12. The King gives the audience some insight into his own guilty conscience in an aside (lines 57–62). What does this admission tell us about Claudius? Does this show that Claudius is not entirely evil?

13. Polonius makes a number of misjudgments in this scene. What are they? How does he try to restore the King's confidence in him in lines 188-190?

14. In their conversation with the King do Rosencrantz and Guildenstern show any animosity toward Hamlet? What is their attitude toward him and toward Claudius?

15. The King uses the term "lawful espials" and the Queen readily agrees to his plan to spy on Hamlet. What might this tell about her character? What justification might there be for this second spy plan? (Remember that Rosencrantz and Guildenstern are already on the job. Spying is not uncommon in *Hamlet*. Reynaldo, at this moment, may be off in Paris spying on Laertes!)

16. How does Hamlet's treatment of Ophelia change as the scene progresses? There have been many explanations of this change. Some productions actually have Hamlet notice a movement of Polonius and the King behind the draperies, but there is no actual warrant for this in the play. Perhaps Hamlet suspects the coincidence that Ophelia happens to have the gifts with her ready to return them. One critic has suggested that Hamlet overheard the plot in the first place. How might you explain his change?

17. What further insights into Ophelia's character do we gain from the conversation with Hamlet? Since she has earlier rejected Hamlet by order of Polonius, why is she surprised when Hamlet seems to reject her?

STAGING AND DIRECTING

18. A crucial element in the staging of this scene is to provide that Polonius and the King may be able to spy on Hamlet. In some versions the King and Polonius are visible to the audience during their eavesdropping. In other versions they are offstage, unseen. Which version do you prefer? Why?

19. How would you place Ophelia on the stage so that Hamlet does not see her as he enters and delivers his famous soliloquy?

INTERPRETATION

20. The side of himself that Claudius shows to Gertrude is always tender and solicitous. How would you read lines 32–41 to suggest his warm feelings toward his wife? Then read lines 174–188 to suggest a subtle difference in tone and feeling.

21. Lines 49–56 give the actor playing Polonius a chance to vary his performance. He speaks alternately to his daughter and to his King and Queen. How should his tone change as he turns from one to the other?

22. How would you read lines 58–62 to suggest the momentary remorse of a hard and cruel man?

23. Polonius tries desperately to justify himself in lines 188–190. How would you read this speech to suggest Polonius's sorrowful recognition of his own misjudgment of the situation. In lines 193–200, what change of tone would you suggest as Polonius grasps one last straw in his effort to restore his King's confidence in him?

24. The *fourth* soliloquy of Hamlet, lines 64–98, is an actor's dream — and an actor's curse. It is a dream because it gives the actor an opportunity to show his talents. It is a curse because of its familiarity. Everyone who knows anything about *Hamlet* knows about this soliloquy. Many persons know it by heart. Indeed, one problem faced by actors is overhearing some people in the front rows saying the words aloud before the actors do. Many actors look toward this soliloquy with some misgiving.

Though it is the most often quoted soliloquy, it may lack some of the dramatic intensity of at least two other soliloquies. This is a quiet, reflective, philosophical aside that does relatively little to advance the action. It gives us insight into Hamlet's mind and it does end with the word *action*. Perhaps this is a prelude to action. Its purpose has, however, been debated. Most critics see it as a consideration of suicide and the reasons for rejecting it. For help in deciding upon your own interpretation, listen to two different recordings if possible.

Considering the possibilities as you now see them, how would you begin the soliloquy? What is the predominant emotional tone with which the opening lines of the soliloquy should be spoken?

25. Harry Levin has pointed out that the word *question* appears in line 64 and in sixteen other places within the play. *Hamlet* is indeed a play of questions — of Hamlet's and our own. What question opens the play? Why is there a question mark in the middle of line 84 and at the end of line 90? What is the basic question that Hamlet is raising? How would you read lines 78–90?

26. The language beginning with "Are you honest?" in line 113 suggests a complete change in tone. Hamlet's attitude toward Ophelia changes. Has he become aware of the spies, as John Dover Wilson suggests? Has he suddenly suspected her motives? Coleridge suggested that Hamlet suddenly realizes that Ophelia is acting a part here and is not herself. Whatever the reason, there is a break. How would you read lines 99–118?

27. The great Ophelias have made much of lines 126 and 130. The interpretation suggests the depth of Ophelia's characterization. What emotions should the actress playing Ophelia suggest here?

28. Hamlet's ominous "all but one, shall live" in line 160 is a sharp and dramatic line. How should it be read? Does Hamlet realize he is saying this for the King's benefit?

LANGUAGE AND IMAGERY

29. Shakespeare's mastery of irony is again revealed, this time in Polonius's lines about deception. (lines 53–56) Which major character in the play has used "pious action" to "sugar o'er the devil himself"? Has Polonius himself engaged in deception?

30. In Hamlet's soliloquy (lines 64–98) he mentions "The undiscover'd country from whose bourn no traveler returns," in other words, the land of the dead. In what sense has he actually met such a traveler? Is he again doubting the reality of the Ghost?

31. Why is "to sleep," line 72, repeated in the next line? Note that "sleep" is again repeated in line 74.

32. In lines 91–93, Hamlet says that conscience (thinking) makes cowards of us all. He compares resolution (decisive action) to health — and thought to sickness. How has this statement actually applied to Hamlet? To what extent is he right in so condemning himself? (Bear in mind that Claudius, Gertrude, Polonius, and Ophelia have all been governed by action rather than thought.)

33. What are some of the burdens of life that Hamlet mentions (lines 78–82)? How do they apply specifically to Hamlet? Are these problems today also? Explain.

34. As Harry Levin points out, the expression *no more*, line 69, occurs like a mournful refrain throughout *Hamlet*. It appears in Laertes' speech and Ophelia's reply. (Act I, Scene 3, lines 11–13) It appears three times in the scene in the Queen's room as she tries to stop Hamlet from criticizing her. (Act III, Scene 4, lines 97, 105, 114) It appears in the graveyard scene in the disagreement between Laertes and the priest. (Act V, Scene 1, lines 228–229) As you read the rest of the play, note how the phrase reappears. What is the effect of the phrase upon you?

35. What does Ophelia mean in the famous line, "Rich gifts wax poor when givers prove unkind"? (line 111)

36. When Hamlet asks Ophelia, "Where's your father?" she replies, "At home, my lord," but of course he is only a few feet away. Why may Hamlet have suddenly asked this question? How would you have Ophelia read her key line — is she nervous, hesitant, bold, or cool as she says this lie?

37. In her speech, lines 162–166, Ophelia tells us what kind of person Hamlet was before the death of King Hamlet. What was he like?

38. Explain the image of the bells in line 170.

39. Notice the rhyming couplet at the end of the scene. How do the King's words suggest a further obstacle for Hamlet?

40. Lines 176–179 demonstrate again the fertility of Shakespeare's imagination and his ability to pour out appropriate figurative language. Analyze these lines closely. What is the comparison that Shakespeare is suggesting here?

Act III, Scene 2

This scene is a crucial one because it contains the play scene. Hamlet decides that it was truly "an honest Ghost." Hamlet's staged play ends the uncertainty about the truth of the elder Hamlet's death. The scene also sets the stage for tragedy when Guildenstern and Rosencrantz summon Hamlet to the Queen's room. It is also in this scene that the two major antagonists, Claudius and Hamlet, come openly face to face with their mutual hatred.

PLOT

1. Polonius, Rosencrantz, and Guildenstern enter together after the advice to the players. Hamlet considers all three his antagonists in one sense or another. Are they likewise bitterly opposed to him? (As you go along, notice how each one of these minor characters plays a crucial role in the plot, and how he suffers for it.)

2. Why is Hamlet presenting this particular play?

3. On three occasions Shakespeare stops the action of the play to comment on the theater of his day. The third time occurs when Hamlet gives his famous advice to the players. (lines 1–46) Where else does this delay with commentary occur?

4. Hamlet makes the murderer in the play scene the *nephew* of the murdered King, not the brother. Why? What mistaken message may the members of the court get from the play?

5. How similar to the actual murder, as revealed by the Ghost, is the murder in the play? What differences are there?

6. The dumb show really "tells all," but the King doesn't seem to notice. In fact, the King says very little in this scene. He welcomes Hamlet. (line 95) He replies briefly to a Hamlet comment. (lines 98–99) He asks two brief questions during the actual play.

(lines 231, 234) He cries out for lights. (line 266) Thus in a very long and crucial scene he has only about five lines. Is there some dramatic advantage in his silences? What might these silences suggest?

7. Rosencrantz and Guildenstern seem truly baffled by Hamlet's actions. Is there any reason for them to understand why Hamlet acts so strangely?

8. Hamlet's soliloquy (lines 380–391) is the fifth of the play. Does this one give us more information about Hamlet's projected course of action than the previous ones? What attitude does he propose to take toward his mother?

CHARACTERIZATION

9. Hamlet's words to Horatio (lines 55–76) are a fine tribute to friendship. What does Hamlet particularly like in Horatio? Does Horatio seem to merit such praise? Does Hamlet possess any of the qualities he praises Horatio for? How does Hamlet's thinking on "blood and judgment" and the "man that is not passion's slave" contrast with thoughts he has expressed elsewhere?

10. How does Hamlet's attitude toward Horatio differ from his attitude toward Rosencrantz and Guildenstern? How do they differ from Horatio? Note that lines 62–64 describe Rosencrantz and Guildenstern from Hamlet's point of view.

11. How is Polonius further made fun of in this scene? (In this scene Hamlet taunts his three minor adversaries, Polonius, Rosencrantz, and Guildenstern.)

12. Why does Hamlet seem to pay attention to Ophelia once again?

13. In what state of mind is Hamlet as the performance begins?

14. How does line 179 remind us of Hamlet's continuing bitterness toward Claudius and Gertrude?

15. Why does the Queen say, "The lady doth protest too much, methinks"? (line 229) How does this line tell us that the Queen probably has a guilty conscience?

16. Why is the King so deeply affected by the play?

17. What does line 264 ("How fares my lord?") tell us about the Queen's affection for Claudius?

18. What does the soliloquy (lines 380–391) tell us about Hamlet's mood after the play?

STAGING AND DIRECTING

19. This scene raises an important question often debated by critics. If the dumb show (or pantomime) of the play really gives the secret away, why is the King not affected by it? The murder is actually reenacted *twice*. The King is affected only the second time. Why?

One explanation sometimes given is that the King isn't paying attention the first time to the dumb show. If you intended to give this impression, how would you stage the scene? How could you place the stage within a stage so that the King could be conspicuously inattentive?

20. Allardyce Nicoll reminds us that the interest is less on the play than on Claudius's reaction to the play. Therefore, Nicoll says, the King should be most prominently placed. The play is secondary. Do you agree? Why?

21. In Shakespearean times the apron stage had no curtain. Therefore every actor had to come on and go off. A modern production on a picture-frame stage might draw the curtain on the King's terror and then have Hamlet and Horatio walk on in the next scene. What advantage in tempo does the Shakespearean stage give the playwright?

22. In the Burton *Hamlet*, Gertrude laughs at Hamlet's bitter jest in lines 96–97. How does this bit of stage business suggest that Gertrude is uneasy at the rift between Hamlet and Claudius?

23. The Burton *Hamlet* also calls for laughter after the Queen's line 229. Why might a director introduce this interpretation, even though there is no suggestion in the text of such an effect?

24. In the Scofield *Hamlet*, lines 235–241 are raced through at breakneck speed. How might such an interpretation suggest Hamlet's mood and emotions at this time?

INTERPRETATION

25. In Hamlet's tribute to Horatio, he seems to pause in the middle of line 76. Some actors suggest that Hamlet is a little self-conscious at the way he has been pouring his heart out. They try to suggest the self-consciousness by changing the tone as they say, "Something too much of this." How would you handle this speech if you were playing Hamlet?

26. The King meets Hamlet for the first time after his decision to send Hamlet to England. How would you deliver line 95?

27. Polonius still hopes that Hamlet loves Ophelia. How should he deliver line 111?

28. What is the effect of a pause after *tell* in line 140?

29. When Hamlet says, "If she should break it now" (line 222), he conveys a great deal of meaning to the audience and to the Queen. How would you deliver this key line?

30. The King's reaction to the play is crucial. How would you deliver lines 231 and 234? Would you give some indication that the King is worried? How?

31. Actors often pause after *Lucianus* in line 242 and then emphasize *nephew.* Why?

32. John Gielgud says that when Rosencrantz and Guildenstern address Hamlet in line 292, they are both very nervous and frightened. They want to get this interview over with as quickly as possible. Do you agree? How should the dialogue be presented?

33. In most productions of *Hamlet,* Polonius looks like a complete fool in the byplay with Hamlet, lines 369–379. He is the obsequious courtier who will *yes* his superior to death on any occasion. Hume Cronyn played this scene differently, however; his Polonius had a controlled irritation usually missing in other versions. He went along with Hamlet's "wit" coolly and curtly. Note that this gives an entirely new dimension to Polonius. Which interpretation do you think preferable here? How do *you* see Polonius at this point?

34. Lines 328 and 329 show a contrast between Hamlet and Rosencrantz. How would you read these two lines? Hamlet's bitter treatment of Guildenstern with the recorder allows for some fine dramatic interpretation. How would you read lines 343–365?

35. Is the dominant tone of Hamlet's soliloquy (lines 380–391) one of anger, exhilaration, despair? How does it contrast with the "To be" soliloquy? What tone should the actor suggest?

LANGUAGE AND IMAGERY

36. The language of the advice-to-the-players scene is famous for its rich imagery and its excellent advice. What lines particularly seem to offer good advice to actors?

37. Hamlet says that during the play scene his eyes will "rivet" to the King's face. Why is this an effective image? Where should Hamlet's attention be during the play scene? (But remember that Ophelia first cries out!)

38. Notice that the language of the Player King and Player Queen are different from the language of Claudius and Gertrude. How does the language differ?

Act III, Scene 3

This scene is notable for the two contrasting soliloquies, by Claudius and Hamlet. In this scene the two antagonists are revealed to us most keenly and sharply. To some critics the failure of Hamlet to kill Claudius is the climax of the play. His reasons for failing to do so are ironic.

This scene also reminds us that Hamlet must go to his mother's room and then to England.

PLOT

1. Notice how three little scenes are compressed into one, with the King as the unifying character in each. With whom does Claudius play each of these scenes? What three developments — all affecting Hamlet — occur?

2. The climax of a play is the turning point. At the climax, events become irreversible. At the climax the audience begins to sense the conclusion, or denouement. It is like climbing a steep hill and then looking down on the other side. Identification of the climax of a play is not always settled beyond dispute. There are three points in the play each often referred to as the climax of *Hamlet*. The first is the play scene, at which the King reveals himself as a murderer. The second is the present scene, in which

Hamlet fails to kill Claudius. The third is the killing of Polonius in the next scene. These three situations come very close together. As you read this and the next scene, try to decide for yourself which of the three situations is indeed the climax. Which one makes the events irreversible?

3. How will Polonius take part in the coming scene between Hamlet and Gertrude? (When Polonius says, lines 36–37, "I'll call upon you ere you go to bed, and tell you what I know," he is promising something he won't be able to deliver.)

4. As we have seen, Hamlet is in a bind because he cannot legally and morally avenge a murder that few people realize is a murder. Claudius, too, is in a bind, though it is of a slightly different kind. He cannot repent *and* keep the fruits of his crime. Both Hamlet and Claudius are intelligent enough to realize the nature of the bind they are both in. Which predicament seems to you the most difficult to face and solve?

CHARACTERIZATION

5. The King is a worthy foe. He has just been upset by the play scene, but here he is in full command of himself and ready to take measures against Hamlet. What are they?

6. The play has forced Claudius to face his sin directly. How does the King most fully reveal himself in his soliloquy? The King may be evil, but he is not self-deceived. How does he show that he recognizes the depths of his crime?

7. How does Polonius again reveal himself as a busybody? Note that in line 32 he says, "As you said." Actually this was Polonius's idea all the way. Why phrase it as he did?

8. How do Rosencrantz and Guildenstern justify their actions on behalf of the King? (In Shakespearean times the King was considered more than just a human being. Murder of a King was a crime against the divine order.)

9. Why does Hamlet refrain from killing Claudius at this point?

STAGING AND DIRECTING

10. The set for this scene usually contains some kind of private shrine for the King's prayer. Why is it important to keep the praying King visible during Hamlet's soliloquy?

11. In many productions the actor playing Hamlet begins to draw his sword with line 76 and then sheathes it again. What value does this bit of business have?

INTERPRETATION

12. In his study of *Hamlet* the great scholar A. C. Bradley italicizes "us" in line 1 of this scene. Should this word be emphasized or would such emphasis be too obvious and self-defeating?

13. The two contrasting soliloquies by Claudius and Hamlet provide ideal possibilities for interpretation. The King is revealed here more clearly than anywhere else because he is speaking honestly — to himself and to the audience. If you were the actor, would you make the King's soliloquy cynical, despairing, bitter, indifferent? Would you represent the King as wishing truly to be able to repent?

14. Hamlet must suggest irony in his soliloquy, the sixth in the play. How, for example, would you read lines 76–81? At what point will your voice change from resolution to ironical restraint? (Richard Burton read "so am I revenged" almost as a question.)

15. How does the King deliver the final two lines of the scene?

LANGUAGE AND IMAGERY

16. Rosencrantz pays tribute to the King and the responsibilities of kingship in lines 12–24. To what does Rosencrantz compare the king's duties and responsibilities?

17. Notice the figure of speech in the King's reply to Rosencrantz and Guildenstern. (lines 26–27) What does he compare fear to?

18. In the King's soliloquy, why does he refer to a brother's murder as having the oldest curse on it (lines 39–41)?

19. In his inner thoughts, at least, Claudius shows in his intelligence and honesty that he is a blood relative to Hamlet. What realistic view of his own success does he present (lines 60–67)? How is his thinking here similar to Hamlet's?

20. Hamlet says, "And how his audit stands who knows save heaven?" What has the Ghost already told Hamlet about the Ghost's difficulties in the afterlife?

21. The medieval concept of heaven as "above" and hell as "below" is vividly pictured in the image in line 96. How?

Act III, Scene 4

This is the Queen's greatest scene, even though she has only a little more than forty lines. Here we come to learn what Gertrude is really like. We gain sharper insights into Hamlet's attitude toward her. In the bitter exchange between mother and son, we learn all over again what the tragedy is all about.

This is a crucial scene for the development of plot. Hamlet kills Polonius and turns his back upon any possibility of reconciliation. The Ghost appears for the last time in the play to spur Hamlet to revenge. Hamlet reminds us that he is going to England.

PLOT

1. How does the death of Polonius make reconciliation between Hamlet and the King impossible?
2. In line 34 Hamlet mentions the phrase, "kill a king." Why doesn't Gertrude realize that Hamlet is accusing her husband of murder? Or if she does, why doesn't she take the charge seriously?
3. In lines 59–60 the Queen asks Hamlet what she has done to merit such abuse. Doesn't she realize what is bothering Hamlet?
4. Hamlet must be momentarily upset, for he asks, "Is it the King?" (line 31) If he had been thinking, he would have realized it could not have been the King. Why?
5. At the very moment when Hamlet seems to be breaking Gertrude down, the Ghost appears. This appearance not only changes Hamlet's attitude; it also changes Gertrude's. She persuades herself that Hamlet is mad; therefore what he says must be madness. Hamlet sees the danger (lines 161–163), but Gertrude seems to want to believe in Hamlet's madness. In a sense, then, how does the Ghost's appearance have a negative effect on the action? (Note that Hamlet has been describing his father at length — and in his spirit comes.)

6. Gertrude cannot see the Ghost. In earlier scenes the Ghost was visible to others as well as Hamlet. Some critics assert that a ghost, traditionally, can choose those to whom he makes himself visible. Others suggest that the Ghost this time is a hallunication of Hamlet's. Yet the Ghost actually has lines to speak. How do you interpret the Ghost's presence in this scene?

7. Hamlet reminds the audience that he is going to England. This trip has been well prepared for dramatically. The King has told us in Act III, Scene 1. He has told us again in Act III, Scene 3. And now in Scene 4 Hamlet reminds us, although we don't know how Hamlet found out. How does Hamlet suggest that he has made appropriate counter-plans?

8. Hamlet urges Gertrude to reject Claudius from this moment on. How does she respond?

CHARACTERIZATION

9. How does Polonius reveal his character again in his last bit of advice to Gertrude?

10. How does the Queen's attitude toward Hamlet change during the course of the scene? At what point in the scene does her attitude change?

11. Hamlet is often accused of being *too* thoughtful, of failing to act because he thinks too much. In this scene he kills Polonius on an impulse. After the deed he doesn't regret his action unduly. Do you feel that Hamlet is a dreamer, as some critics suggest, or a man of action who has been restrained by force and by conscience? What indication is there that Hamlet thought he was killing Claudius?

12. Why is the Queen's conscience guilty? (lines 97–107) (Remember: she is not involved in the murder.)

13. How do lines 125–128 provide indications that Hamlet's father deeply loved Gertrude? We have had a similar indication in lines 91–94 of Act I, Scene 5.

14. At times Hamlet seems more upset by his mother's hasty marriage than by his father's murder. How does this scene support that impression?

15. How much does Hamlet trust Rosencrantz and Guildenstern?

16. Why does the Ghost reappear in this scene? Critics have debated whether or not this is the same spirit we have met earlier. Are there indications that this is the same Ghost we met earlier in the play?

STAGING AND DIRECTING

17. This, of course, is an altogether new scene: the Queen's apartment, sometimes called the "Queen's closet." How would you provide for the spying of Polonius in this scene? Would you have him visible to the audience as he spies? Why or why not? The arras is a huge tapestry hung close to the wall but not touching it. The purpose of the arras was to keep the drafty castle warmer and drier.

18. When Hamlet compares the former King to the present King, he refers to two pictures. Some productions actually have pictures on the walls. Others use lockets. Hamlet has a locket with his father's picture; Gertrude has a locket with Claudius's picture. Which device do you prefer?

19. From time to time Shakespeare does provide assistance for the director of a play. In the text itself he provides clues to the characters' actions. How does line 40, for example, help the director?

20. When the Ghost appears in this scene, he is away from the gloomy parapets of the castle. How would you introduce the Ghost into this lighted scene and still keep the air of dread and mystery associated with him?

21. When the Ghost appears, where should the Queen be looking? Some actresses who play Gertrude look wildly around the room like Hamlet and seem like him in emotional upset. Other Gertrudes glance quickly around the room only once and then keep their eyes on Hamlet very closely. If you were the director, how would you suggest the actress play the Ghost scene?

INTERPRETATION

22. What kind of person is Gertrude? Vain? Proud? Strong-willed? Basically weak? Immature despite her years? There are many possibilities and combinations of possibilities. The interpretation of Gertrude's character takes life from this scene. Up to this point Gertrude has had relatively little to say. (Even in this scene her lines are vastly outnumbered by Hamlet's.) In this scene the actress portraying Gertrude must make up her mind about Gertrude. Select several of her lines and decide how *you* would deliver them. Lines 97–100, 105–107, and 130–138 are particularly important.

23. The mother-son dialogue in lines 9–20 is realistic. In a sense these are "games people play." Gertrude is playing the role of the aggrieved mother. Hamlet is playing the disrespectful son. How should these lines be read? What words would you emphasize in lines 10–15?

24. What are the various changes in Hamlet's mood throughout this scene?

25. Try reading the key lines 70–71 and 79. What words would you emphasize?

26. The Ghost has six lines (123–128). His speech is in two parts. The first reminds Hamlet of his revenge. The second concerns Gertrude. What possible difference in tone might there be between these two parts?

27. How does Hamlet read his lines (221–224) about Rosencrantz and Guildenstern? About Polonius? (lines 232–234)

LANGUAGE AND IMAGERY

28. In his comparison of the elder Hamlet and Claudius, Hamlet uses some of the most vivid language in the play. Hamlet was like a god, Claudius is a "mildew'd ear." What other comparison does he bring into his vivid speech?

29. Explain the metaphor Hamlet uses (lines 90–93) to condemn Gertrude's behavior.

30. With what words does the Queen admit to having a spotted soul?

31. Hamlet's descriptions of the King throughout the play have been more and more unflattering. In lines 108–113 he climaxes his attack. What does he say here to disrobe Claudius of the majesty of kingship and show him in his true dimensions?

32. Shakespeare provides few stage directions, but in the characters' lines he tells us what is going on. According to the Queen (lines 130–136), what does Hamlet look like here?

33. Hamlet says, "I must be cruel only to be kind." What are some common human situations where honesty may be necessary, however cruel?

Act IV, Scene 1

In this scene the King learns the extent of his own danger when he is told about the death of Polonius. Somehow the King must protect himself and still keep the love and confidence of Gertrude, who loves Hamlet. The King reacts with force and skill.

PLOT

1. The King says (line 31), "We will ship him hence." The King had already decided to send Hamlet to England, as we have been told. But now the departure has a special urgency. Why?

2. Why is there anxiety in the King's "You must translate"? (line 2) Whom is he addressing this line to? What information is he seeking?

3. How does the King show his power over Hamlet in line 34?

CHARACTERIZATION

4. Why hasn't the Queen told Claudius about Polonius's death? She tells only when Claudius asks point blank, "Where is your son?" (Not *our* son!)

5. The Queen continues to harp on Hamlet's madness. Is her description of Hamlet's actions, lines 7–12, an accurate report? She also says that Hamlet "weeps for what is done." Is this true? Why does she say it?

6. How does line 14 show us that the King now realizes the danger he is in?

7. The King's explanation of his aims, lines 31–33, is purely for Gertrude's benefit. Why?

8. Why does the King say that he will seek advice (lines 39–45) about explaining the death of Polonius? Remember that in Act I, Scene 2, the King indicated that he had asked his courtiers' advice about marrying Gertrude. (lines 14–16)

9. Note that the King's major concern seems to be that he, Claudius, will be blamed for giving Hamlet too much leeway. (lines 18–24) Is the speech partly for Gertrude's benefit?

STAGING AND DIRECTING

10. In one production of *Hamlet,* as Gertrude and Claudius go out, Gertrude hesitates for a moment and then goes off in a direction opposite to that of the King. This director's touch suggests that Gertrude has taken Hamlet's advice to reject the King. Is there anything in the play itself to suggest this interpretation, or is this purely a director's own idea? How far should a director go in introducing rather basic interpretations of this kind? What responsibilities, if any, does a director have toward the original playwright of any play? What freedoms must he inevitably take? In producing an older play for a new and different society, what can or should the director do to make the older play seem up to date?

INTERPRETATION

11. A key line in this scene is 14. How should the King deliver this line, in which he realizes that *he* might have been killed?

12. The Queen's speeches emphasize Hamlet's madness — for his protection. Notice that the King picks up this cue (line 35) and says that Hamlet slew Polonius "in madness." How would you read this line? Does Claudius really dismiss the slaying as mere madness?

13. How would you read the final line of this scene? What is the King's mood at this moment?

LANGUAGE AND IMAGERY

14. The Queen's descriptions of Hamlet's madness are poetic. She compares his madness to a storm. (lines 7–8) She says that his regret is like some pure ore in base minerals. (lines 26–28) Have we had any evidence of Hamlet's tearful regret at the killing of Polonius?

15. How does the King compare his own tolerance of Hamlet's madness with a disease that people try to cover up? (lines 22–24)

16. What is slander compared to in lines 41–45? Why is the air called "woundless"?

Act IV, Scene 2

This scene provides an immediate sequel to the death of Polonius and to the King's command that Rosencrantz and Guildenstern find Hamlet. It prepares us for a new confrontation between Hamlet and Claudius, and builds suspense. When these two meet again, the lines will be clearly drawn. Each man will more keenly understand the nature of his antagonist. As king, Claudius has the upper hand, of course. He has the throne — and the power.

PLOT

1. Is this scene essential to the plot? Could it be dropped from a production without loss? Does it add anything to the play?

2. What are Rosencrantz and Guildenstern requesting of Hamlet? What is his reply?

CHARACTERIZATION

3. Gertrude has just said in the previous scene that Hamlet "weeps for what is done." Is there any evidence in this scene that Hamlet has wept for what he did? What is Hamlet's mood here? How can you explain it?

4. Why do Rosencrantz and Guildenstern still try to handle Hamlet gently? Is there any change in their behavior toward Hamlet?

5. What is Hamlet's attitude toward his two former friends? Why does he scorn them?

STAGING AND DIRECTING

6. Some productions actually have Hamlet dragging the body of Polonius as he enters. Is there any value in such a device? Any danger?

INTERPRETATION

7. Notice that the replies of Rosencrantz are brief and courteous. Are they, however, colorless lines, or should they be read with some specific interpretation in mind?
8. Guildenstern says only one line (28), but it is a line clearly indicating surprise. How should this line be read?

LANGUAGE AND IMAGERY

9. The basic image in Hamlet's speech is that of a sponge. (lines 15–20) What characteristics of the sponge does Rosencrantz have? What fate will he suffer, according to Hamlet?
10. Critics have pointed out Shakespeare's preoccupation with life as a jungle in which various life forms prey on others. What evidences of such preoccupation are there in this scene?

Act IV, Scene 3

This is an important scene because the King reveals to the audience that he intends to have Hamlet killed. Up to this point we have known only that the King feels unsafe with Hamlet around. We have also realized that Claudius could not act directly against Hamlet because of Gertrude. But now Claudius feels he *must* get rid of Hamlet. Somehow he will explain to Gertrude. Knowing his skill in diplomacy, we can believe he will succeed.

PLOT

1. How does the audience now realize that this is a struggle to the death between Claudius and Hamlet?

2. Is Hamlet surprised that he is being sent to England? (line 51) Or does the question mark suggest a different emotion? In what earlier scene did Hamlet tell us that he was being sent to England?

3. Why does the King say, "Tempt him with speed aboard," (line 59) and "Pray you, make haste"? (line 62)

4. Why does the King expect England to kill Hamlet for him? Why should the King of England perform this unpleasant task?

CHARACTERIZATION

5. The King is a clever diplomat. How does he show his skill in diplomacy in the opening lines?

6. What is the attitude of the common folk toward Hamlet? (line 4) Does their judgment correspond with the judgment by the audience?

7. What pose does Hamlet seem to put on when he is brought before Claudius?

8. Lines 49–52 are often debated. Why does Hamlet say "Good" when told about his enforced trip to England? And why does the King tip his hand slightly in line 52? Why are these antagonists so open and obvious to each other?

9. How does Hamlet continue to show his contempt for Claudius, as in lines 56–58?

10. In the King's soliloquy (lines 63–73) how does he demonstrate his ability to strike back at Hamlet? Why doesn't he act more directly, right at home in Denmark?

STAGING AND DIRECTING

11. Why didn't Shakespeare include Gertrude in this scene?

12. When Hamlet appears this time, he is surrounded by soldiers. What line prepares us for this change? Also reread line 34 of Act IV, Scene 1.

13. Why are Rosencrantz and Guildenstern separated briefly in this scene? They are rarely apart otherwise.

INTERPRETATION

14. Though this is a bleak scene, it always gets a number of laughs. The lines that always seem most grimly humorous to the audience are 35–39, 41, and 54. How should these lines be read?

15. Line 31 is a key line. It may suggest anxiety, bravado, concern, or some other emotion. How would you read it?

16. The King's speeches, at the beginning of the scene and the end, are filled with clues for interpretation of the character. It is in scenes like these that the actor playing Claudius most sharply determines the characterization he is building. How would you read these two speeches?

17. Hamlet's answers to Claudius are close to treason, as he talks about a king's mortality. How should this dialogue (lines 19–58) be read?

LANGUAGE AND IMAGERY

18. The gloomy imagery of death and decay floods the speech of Hamlet in this scene, as it does in the graveyard scene to come. Yet it seems to get laughs from every audience. Why?

19. Claudius compares Hamlet to a fever ("hectic") in his blood. Is this an effective image under the circumstances?

Act IV, Scene 4

One major purpose of this scene seems to be to provide an opportunity for an important Hamlet soliloquy. It also reminds us that Hamlet is on his way to England. And it refreshes our memories by bringing in Fortinbras in the flesh. Since Fortinbras will appear at the end of the play, an appearance beforehand is desirable. Here it is.

PLOT

1. In his soliloquy, the seventh and last of the play, Hamlet berates himself for inaction. Yet when we last saw him, he was under guard. He could not have attacked the King then. Why, then, does he continue to blame himself?

2. This scene was prepared for in the agreement between Claudius and the old King of Norway. (Act II, Scene 2, lines 76–84) How?

3. This scene also reminds the audience that Hamlet is going to England. Is this reminder necessary at this point?

4. Lines 46–48 have been offered as proof by those critics who say that Hamlet had opportunities to kill Claudius, but failed to take advantage of them. Bernard Grebanier insists that Hamlet never really had a chance to do so. Is there any evidence in the play that Hamlet had an opportunity to kill Claudius — other than the praying scene?

5. The soliloquy does provide another resolution by Hamlet: "From this time forth, my thoughts be bloody, or be nothing worth!" Has he made similar resolutions in the past? Why has he not acted upon them?

6. Notice that Rosencrantz and Guildenstern are still with Hamlet. Why?

CHARACTERIZATION

7. Does Fortinbras's speech give us any indication of his character? How does Hamlet's analysis of Fortinbras give us a better indication of what Fortinbras is like? (lines 50–55)

8. Hamlet understands irony perhaps better than anyone else in the play. He constantly sees the difference between what is and what seems to be. In his soliloquy (lines 34–68) he provides another instance of irony. What is it?

9. The Captain (lines 18–23) truly understands the stupidity of this war between Norway and Poland. Why do the men fight?

10. Scenes 3 and 4 are parallel scenes in certain respects. Each ends with a soliloquy by one of the two antagonists. Both soliloquies tell us a great deal about the two men. How are Claudius and Hamlet again contrasted here and in Scene 3?

STAGING AND DIRECTING

11. Some productions have shadows of marching men thrown against a screen. Others merely have recordings of marching feet played throughout this scene. Tyrone Guthrie placed Fortinbras on a height, in shadow, as Hamlet spoke on the stage. How would you stage this scene?

12. Some productions have omitted this scene altogether. What do you think? Can it be omitted without detracting seriously from the plot? What does it add?

INTERPRETATION

13. The dramatic soliloquy in this scene has been a favorite of actors. It contains anger, bitterness, irony, sarcasm, resolution. In addition, it provides a handy review of the play up to date and a hint of what's to come. How would you read this soliloquy? (Perhaps you can compare recordings to see how different actors have interpreted the lines.)

14. Consider for a moment how each of the soliloquies arises out of a special situation.

Soliloquy 1, lines 131–161 of Act I, Scene 2, arises from Hamlet's disgust at the close relationship between Claudius and Gertrude after their rather hasty marriage.

Soliloquy 2, lines 98–118 of Act 1, Scene 5, arises from the Ghost's disclosure of the murder.

Soliloquy 3, lines 555-613 of Act II, Scene 2, arises from the player's emotional rendition of the lines about Hecuba and the Trojan victims of Greek cruelty.

Soliloquy 4, lines 64–98 of Act III, Scene 1, arises from Hamlet's contemplation of the ills of life and the uncertainties of the afterlife.

Soliloquy 5, lines 380–391 of Act III, Scene 2, arises from the unmasking of the King at the play scene.

Soliloquy 6, lines 76–99 of Act III, Scene 3, arises from Hamlet's finding the King at his prayers.

Soliloquy 7, lines 34–68 of Act IV, Scene 4, arises from Hamlet's evaluation of Fortinbras's motives and actions.

Do you feel that these soliloquies add to the plot? Which is your favorite? Which seems most dramatic to you?

LANGUAGE AND IMAGERY

15. Where in this scene does Shakespeare seem to be presenting antiwar speeches?

16. How does Hamlet again blame thinking too much for his inaction?

17. How does Hamlet contrast himself and Fortinbras? To whose advantage is the comparison?

18. The war will not gain enough ground to bury the dead. What is Hamlet's purpose in making this comment?

Act IV, Scene 5

This is Ophelia's most important and most difficult scene. Her madness contributes to the complexities of the plot. Laertes returns, presenting a threat to the King. The King must somehow turn aside Laertes' rage, and still retain the love of Gertrude. At this point the King thinks he has taken care of Hamlet.

Although Hamlet is onstage in nearly all of the play, he is offstage during this scene and the next two. As John Gielgud has said, at this point Hamlet gets ten minutes in the dressing room. This absence of Hamlet adds a great deal to the tension, however, since he is very much present in everyone's mind.

PLOT

1. How is Scene 5 a logical extension of all the action up to this point? Shakespeare rarely introduces a plot element without preparation. How has Shakespeare prepared us, even before this scene, for the madness of Ophelia and the entrance of Laertes?

2. How does Shakespeare prepare us in this scene itself for the madness of Ophelia? Notice that he adds the King's commentary for our benefit. (lines 76–86)

3. Notice how skillfully and realistically Shakespeare removes Horatio and Ophelia in the middle of the scene. Why is it dramatically important to allow Claudius and Gertrude to speak together and alone at this point?

4. How does Shakespeare prepare us in this scene for the rage of Laertes? (lines 87–91)

5. What promise does the King make to Laertes in lines 217–231? Why is the King secure in making such a promise?

6. Laertes objects to the secrecy with which Polonius was buried. How can Claudius explain this seeming insult?

7. The King has three main problems: to quiet down the infuriated Laertes; to tell Laertes that Hamlet is the villain; and to keep the love of Gertrude. These problems suggest conflicting solutions. Yet the King manages all three! Why does he not try to get Laertes to promise to kill Hamlet at this point?

8. Why does Shakespeare have Ophelia come in twice? Why not keep her on stage throughout?

CHARACTERIZATION

9. Ophelia has never demonstrated great strength of character. Thus her madness here is not completely unexpected. There is never any question about the actuality of her insanity. What two roots of her madness are revealed by her songs?

10. How does Laertes change in this scene? What had been his attitude toward the King in his last meeting with him?

11. How do lines 120 and 135 show that Gertrude probably still loves Claudius? Remember that she also has a stake in the throne, and her fate is very much tied to that of Claudius.

12. This scene shows Claudius at his skillful best. How does he cleverly quiet down Laertes?

13. How do Laertes' actions contrast with Hamlet's when they are both faced with the violent deaths of their fathers?

14. How does this scene contrast the characters of Laertes and Claudius? Who is the more intelligent? More skillful? More crafty?

15. How does the King increase his hold over Gertrude by saying how much he has done to preserve Hamlet?

16. Commentators have called the Queen cruel for at first refusing to speak to Ophelia. (line 1) Others have said she is shallow, unwilling to face bitter reality. What might be the Queen's reasons for not wishing to see Ophelia now? Who finally insists that Ophelia be allowed to come in? What sound reasons does he offer? What is the Queen's attitude toward Ophelia once she has entered?

STAGING AND DIRECTING

17. Most productions of Hamlet take advantage of the entrance of Laertes to change the mood. The first entrance of Ophelia is sad. The King and Queen speak softly. Then there is a loud noise. (One production used a loud metallic crash that fairly shook the rafters of the theater.) How does this tension help prepare the audience for Laertes' violent entry?

18. As Laertes rushes in with his followers, all eyes turn to the King. How should he stand as Laertes comes toward him? Should he make any gestures or stand perfectly still?

19. What stage direction does Shakespeare provide for us in lines 127 and 131?

20. Most productions of *Hamlet* show Ophelia throwing flowers about the stage. At least one production had Ophelia enter with a book. She pointed to pictures in the book. Which seems to you the more effective method?

21. There is a change in the dramatic intensity when Ophelia arrives for the second time. Laertes has been excited, shouting, unruly. Then Ophelia enters and a quietness settles on the scene. Is this dramatically effective?

22. Claudius must get Laertes alone to speak with him about the death of Polonius. (They are shown together later in Scene 7.) Why cannot Claudius and Laertes talk openly at this point? Why do we need another scene altogether?

INTERPRETATION

23. The Queen's opening line is most significant. Does she feel guilty? Irritated? Fearful? Indifferent? How would you read the line?

24. Ophelia's "mad speeches" are difficult for any actress. Why? What are the possible pitfalls?

25. How would you interpret Horatio's insistence, lines 15–16? After all, he *is* speaking to the Queen.

26. The Queen confesses to a "sick soul" in line 18. How would you read lines 17–21?

27. The King's speech to Gertrude shows us a different Claudius. He is upset but by no means defeated. Things have been going wrong, and Claudius here takes advantage of the situation to show Gertrude that he has acted partly for her. How would you read this speech?

28. Line 36, "Pray you, mark," is often spoken harshly, interrupting the Queen who has just begun to speak. What is the effect of a harsh tone by Ophelia at this point?

29. Notice that again Claudius mentions the name *Laertes* several times in talking with him. In Act I, Scene 2, he used the same device. What is the intended effect of such repetition?

30. How would you read the King's reaction to Laertes in these lines: 125–132, 134, 136, 144?

31. "I'll not be juggled with," in line 137, is an interesting sentence to play with. What are some of the different ways in which this can be said?

32. Note that it takes a while for the King to respond to Laertes after Laertes has broken in. Why?

33. In a sense Laertes seems easily quieted. He has rushed in, ready to kill the King. He has seen his sister wandering in madness. Yet by the end of the scene he is fairly quiet. How would you read his final speech? (lines 224–229)

34. What attitude does the King take toward Laertes in the King's final lines? (lines 230–232) How do these lines show the King's control over Laertes?

LANGUAGE AND IMAGERY

35. Ophelia's ballads are usually sung on the stage. Should they be?

36. According to the Gentleman, Ophelia's mad words mean different things to different people. (lines 8–14) Would this be likely?

37. How are lines 78–79 similar to the proverb, "It never rains but it pours"?

38. The Gentleman's description of Laertes' arrival vividly describes the actions of the mob. If this description also reflects Shakespeare's attitude toward mobs, how did Shakespeare look upon the mob? (If you have read *Julius Caesar*, show how Shakespeare also expressed an attitude toward mobs in that play.)

39. When the King said, "There's such divinity doth hedge a king" (line 128), Laertes would certainly hesitate. The divine right of kings was a live doctrine at the time Shakespeare wrote. How does Laertes react to the mention of treason, with its suggestion of vows and loyalty?

40. If the greatest grief is wordless, how do Laertes' words on the arrival of Ophelia (lines 166–170) seem somewhat less than overwhelming?

Act IV, Scene 6

This scene has but one purpose: to tell us that Hamlet has been captured by pirates. The fateful trip to England has been avoided, and Hamlet will return home.

PLOT

1. Horatio has served in the past as an agent through whom the audience learns what is happening. How does Horatio serve that purpose here? What do you learn from the letter?

2. What unexpected change in the King's plans are foreshadowed in this scene?

3. Rosencrantz and Guildenstern are continuing for England. Does Hamlet tell us anything further about them in this scene?

4. Hamlet asks that letters be delivered to the King. What immediate effect will the news that Hamlet has returned, unharmed, have on Claudius?

CHARACTERIZATION

5. How does Hamlet once again demonstrate his trust in Horatio?

6. How does Hamlet, in the letter, show that he is a man of action, not a purposeless dreamer?

STAGING AND DIRECTING

7. The stage directions tell us that this is set in "another room in the castle." Why is the setting unimportant for this scene?

8. The Richard Burton *Hamlet* omitted this scene and ran Scenes 5 and 7 together. What do you think of this procedure?

INTERPRETATION

9. The news about Hamlet's capture by pirates is important for the audience. How can Horatio read the letter in a way to ensure that the audience gets the point?

10. Shakespeare provides some clue as to how Horatio receives this news about Hamlet's imminent return. How should Horatio read lines 30–32?

LANGUAGE AND IMAGERY

11. What does Hamlet mean by a "compelled valour"? (line 17)
12. Why does Hamlet say the pirates acted like "thieves of mercy"? (line 20)

Act IV, Scene 7

This scene sets up the final plot against Hamlet. It enlists Claudius and Laertes as co-conspirators. It also gives us the news about Ophelia's death.

As the scene opens, the King feels secure. Hamlet will be taken care of. Laertes is bending to the King's will. Then comes the news of Hamlet's escape. The King has little time to change his strategy and work out a deadly plot against Hamlet. How he does it is a masterpiece of applied psychology.

PLOT

1. There is a brilliant about-face soon after this scene opens. At the beginning the King and Laertes are talking calmly, without any sense of urgency. Then some news comes to change the pace and the mood. What news?

2. Why is the King eager to set up a plot that must be considered an accident? How do he and Laertes plan such a plot? What extra precautions do they plan to take to kill Hamlet? Could death in a fencing match be considered an accident? Is Claudius growing more desperate?

3. Why does the King mention Lamond, the Norman fencer? Do you think his mention of Hamlet's envy is true or manufactured?

4. Why does Shakespeare break the news of Ophelia's death toward the end of this scene, rather than at the beginning?

5. Note how the King is able to turn all news to his advantage. He uses the death of Ophelia to solidify his position with the Queen and further control Laertes. How true is his line, "How much I had to do to calm his rage"? (line 212)

6. Poison as a murder weapon appears twice in the play. What are the two occasions? Who is the poisoner in each?

CHARACTERIZATION

7. How does the King's opening conversation with Laertes show the King in complete command of the situation? How does the King convince Laertes that he, the King, is wise, and powerful?

8. Why is Claudius so concerned when he asks, "Are all the rest come back?" (line 53) Why should that possibility bother him?

9. How does the King show his resourcefulness in lines 63–65 right after the news about Hamlet?

10. Why doesn't the King immediately blurt out his new plot against Hamlet? How does he test Laertes first? How does he lead up to the plot? What pretext does Claudius use for relying on a duel for the revenge? How does this strategy deepen our understanding of Claudius as a character? As a worthy antagonist for Hamlet?

11. Claudius is a superb psychologist in lines 124–137. What does he fear in Laertes' character?

12. How does Laertes show himself easily led by Claudius? How does Laertes show himself willing to play at treachery? How does Laertes' treachery contrast with Hamlet's more open actions?

Laertes tells of buying poison. What does this touch tell us of his character? Can you picture Hamlet buying poison like this?

13. Does the Queen's brief appearance in this scene add anything to our understanding of her character?

14. In a sense Claudius understands Laertes perhaps better than anyone else in the play. What evidence is there for such an assertion?

STAGING AND DIRECTING

15. A new scene seems necessary for the important conversation between Claudius and Laertes. Why must they have a chance to talk *alone*? (Remember that during Hamlet's first conversation with the Ghost a new scene was provided so that Hamlet and the Ghost could be alone.)

16. Why does Ophelia's death occur offstage? After all, there are other forms of dying that could have been managed onstage. (The opening lines of the next scene provide part of the answer.)

17. This scene is necessary for the action but difficult to play. It appears after the dramatic Ophelia and Laertes scene and before the gravedigger scene. It is often cut to shreds in the actual staging; yet it is a masterpiece of psychology and worthy of the audience's attention. If you were directing this scene, would you cut portions of the dialogue? Why or why not?

INTERPRETATION

18. The King's character is further illuminated in this scene. He is a master of subtlety. He knows how to manage people. Indeed, he has managed most of the major characters in the play, except Hamlet. Read aloud the speech (lines 11–26) in which he openly gives Laertes the two reasons for not punishing Hamlet for the death of Polonius. What image of himself does he try to give to Laertes in the way he speaks?

19. Is the King genuinely surprised to hear the news about Hamlet? How would you read line 41? How would you read line 56? Is the King momentarily defeated by this news, or is he merely marking time while his fertile brain considers what to do next?

20. Notice the contrast between Laertes' hotheaded boasting (lines 59–62, 66–67) and Claudius's more deadly calm (lines 63–65, 68–75). How would you read lines 59–76 to show the contrast?

21. What word would you emphasize in line 58: "Can you advise me?" Try emphasizing each in turn.

22. The King comes to the heart of his plot when Laertes asks, "What out of this, my lord?" (line 119) The King still hesitates to tell Laertes outright that he, the King, has a plan to kill Hamlet. And so he tests a little more. How would you read this testing speech (lines 124–140)?

23. If the King emphasizes *was* in line 120, what does the reading tell us about Claudius and Laertes?

24. The Queen's announcement about the death of Ophelia (line 182) and Laertes' recognition of the death (line 183) are two key lines, but they are not easy. How do you think they should be read?

LANGUAGE AND IMAGERY

25. In lines 13–18 the King confesses his love for Gertrude. Is he sincere in his profession of love?

26. How does the King say the public looks upon Hamlet's faults?

27. The King uses a vivid image to suggest the danger he has been in. How does line 34 present this image?

28. There is brilliant irony in the King's lines, 32–37. He is boasting that he has taken care of Hamlet. What then happens to make him "eat his words"?

29. Shakespeare has often commented on the brevity of love. Read lines 125–132 again and point out the comparisons he makes. What does he mean by suggesting there can be too much goodness? (lines 131–132)

30. In the Queen's description of Ophelia's death, Shakespeare paints a word picture that enables each listener to set the stage himself. In the movie version of Hamlet, the audience actually saw Ophelia drowning as the words were being spoken. Which method do you think you might prefer?

Act V, Scene 1

This scene provides a change of tone and pace in the graveyard dialogue. It also brings Hamlet and Laertes together and prepares the way for the fateful duel. Since this is the funeral of Ophelia, the scene helps to bring together many plot elements in preparation for the final scene to follow.

PLOT

1. How does Hamlet happen to be in the graveyard at this time?

2. There is a pause in the rapid development of the plot as the gravediggers joke with Hamlet. Does this pause have dramatic value of any kind?

3. Why does Hamlet have no inkling that the grave is Ophelia's?

4. What threat to the King's plot does Hamlet's too-sudden appearance represent? Notice that the King quickly says, "Pluck them asunder." (line 263)

5. How does the King finally take advantage of the fight in the grave to further his plot?

CHARACTERIZATION

6. The First Clown, sometimes called "First Gravedigger," does provide a kind of grisly comic relief. How is he differentiated from the Second Clown? (Note that the Second Clown goes out for liquor and never returns. One Clown is enough to handle Hamlet!)

7. Two sides of Hamlet are revealed in this scene: the philosopher and the doer. How does he show each of these two sides of his character?

8. Hamlet's evaluation of others tends to be generous. He calls Laertes "a very noble youth." How does this evaluation contrast with our knowledge of Laertes' plotting in the previous scene?

9. How do Hamlet's actions at the grave give us some clue to his real feelings for Ophelia? Why hadn't he shown these feelings to her? (Note that Hamlet unknowingly has been joking over the grave of one he may have loved.)

10. How does the King continue to show his resourcefulness? How does he still strive to keep control of the explosive situation in this scene? How does he take advantage of the situation once again to further his plot?

11. What is the Queen's reason for insisting upon Hamlet's madness? (line 286)

12. Hamlet has killed Laertes' father and helped bring his sister to death by drowning. Yet he says, "I lov'd you ever," and he acts surprised by Laertes' anger? Why?

13. Hamlet reveals a menacing side of his character in lines 259–262. Have we seen this side earlier in the play?

14. Critics have pointed out that except for Horatio, the characters in the play tend to side with Claudius, not Hamlet. The audience, however, tends to side with Hamlet. Why is there this discrepancy?

STAGING AND DIRECTING

15. Productions of *Hamlet* have to solve the graveyard setting. They must provide a space for the struggle between Hamlet and Laertes. They must suggest a graveyard in other ways. Some productions have a raised grave, with Laertes and Hamlet struggling at eye level. Others provide a hole in the stage. Hamlet and Laertes then struggle with just their heads and shoulders visible. If you were staging *Hamlet*, how would you provide for this scene?

16. In one production of *Hamlet*, Maurice Evans eliminated the graveyard scene altogether. He said that it is difficult to play this scene and the one following it in the same play. In this scene Horatio doesn't tell Hamlet for whom the grave is intended, even though he must have known. In the next scene Hamlet talks lightly about his sea experiences as though Act V, Scene 1, had never existed. Thus, Evans says, this scene should go. Of course, many critics disagree violently. Perhaps after you have finished the play, you will decide for yourself: should this scene be cut?

17. The question of Hamlet's age is a burning one with the critics. Just how old is Hamlet anyway? What clues to Hamlet's age can you find in this scene?

Some critics say, "Hamlet is thirty. The play is definite." Others say, "Impossible! He has to be a much younger man. This is a slip." Still others say, "Shakespeare probably started the play with a younger Hamlet in mind and then changed his mind as the play grew in complexity."

No one has the last word, but you are invited to take part. How do *you* picture Hamlet? Do you think only a very young man should be permitted to play the part?

INTERPRETATION

18. In modern stage slang the First Clown is the "top banana" and the Second Clown is the "second banana." Notice that the First Clown gets most of the laughs. The other is his stooge, who feeds him key lines. How is it possible that people laugh at this scene in the midst of a tragedy? Its subject matter is basically not funny. Much of the early part of the scene is done rather lightly. Hamlet and Horatio laugh ruefully at several points.

19. With what tone of voice does Hamlet deliver his philosophical comments about man, life, and death? What attitude does Hamlet take toward the gravediggers?

20. Lines 206–209 were delivered lightly in the Scofield *Hamlet* and seriously in the Burton *Hamlet*. Which interpretation seems better to you?

21. Note the contrast between the Priest's measured response to Laertes and Laertes' own anger. How has Laertes earlier demonstrated this hotheaded side of his personality?

22. In the dialogue between the Priest and Laertes, there are several excellent lines allowing different interpretations. When Laertes says, "What ceremony else?" for the second time (line 218), he is likely to emphasize *else*. Why? When the Priest repeats "No more be done" (line 229), he has several possibilities to choose from. He may read the words as an exclamation, or he may read them as a simple statement. How would each of these possibilities sound? Which would you prefer? If you get the recordings of the Shakespeare Recording Society and the Burton production of *Hamlet*, you will notice subtle differences in these speeches.

23. How does Hamlet deliver the lines, 259–262? How does Horatio deliver the line, 266?

24. Line 272 is a fine line to play with. What is the difference in meaning if we emphasize *do* instead of *thou?*

25. What word would you emphasize in line 279?

26. The King's comments to Laertes are interesting here. How would you read line 273? 297–298?

27. The Queen tries to quiet the angry tumult. How does she deliver lines 286–290?

28. In his final speech, the King addresses three persons in turn: Horatio, Laertes, Gertrude. How does his voice change as he turns to each one?

LANGUAGE AND IMAGERY

29. Critics have often commented on Shakespeare's puns. The First Gravedigger is a real Shakespearean punster, as in line 33. Do you think a pun is out of place in the midst of a tragic play like *Hamlet?* (Remember that in Shakespeare's time the pun had a higher reputation than it does now, though it is likely we pun as much as did the gallants of Shakespeare's day!)

30. How does the Priest indicate, subtly, that influence was brought to bear so that Ophelia could be buried in hallowed ground? (Is Shakespeare possibly objecting to influence from high places?)

31. Once again Shakespeare brings beauty into death as Laertes pays tribute to his sister. (lines 234–235) What tribute does the Queen pay?

32. Does Hamlet's expression of love for Ophelia (lines 270–272) seem somewhat exaggerated in view of his treatment of her? Why or why not?

Act V, Scene 2

In this final scene of the play, the various plot threads are tied together. Hamlet has his revenge at last. The evil in Denmark is wiped out. Morality can reenter in the person of Fortinbras.

Hamlet has his revenge, true. Yet there is an almost accidental quality to the revenge that adds a note of irony to the play. After all the resolutions and missed opportunities, Hamlet kills Claudius at last because events sweep him to it. He recognizes himself, suddenly, as the victim of the fencing plot. He sees his mother's death. Then he acts, decisively. If life tends to have a spontaneous and unexpected quality, then *Hamlet* indeed resembles life. And if people tend to have puzzling, contradictory, unclassifiable natures, then Hamlet resembles a real person. Not one of us can be summed up in a sentence, a paragraph, a page; or a book. Hamlet is no exception.

When Hamlet dies, for most of the audience the play really ends. There is a necessary epilogue in which we learn definitely of the deaths of Rosencrantz and Guildenstern. Fortinbras enters to reestablish some kind of normality. Horatio comments on the death of Hamlet. But when Hamlet says, "The rest is silence," the long vigil we have kept with Hamlet is ended.

PLOT

1. Why did Hamlet send Rosencrantz and Guildenstern to their deaths? In your judgment were their deaths justified? In lines 64–66 Hamlet himself suggests why these men were destroyed. The recent play *Rosencrantz and Guildenstern Are Dead,* by Tom Stoppard, develops the theme of those three lines and shows us two men baffled and buffeted by the events that are swirling around them; the two courtiers are just unfortunates who have fallen in the path of a steamroller. Does Shakespeare allow such an interpretation?

2. One of the most persistent motifs in folklore is that of a young man who is given a letter. The young man does not realize that the letter carries his death warrant. Somehow, in the folktales, the youth realizes the danger he is in and turns the misfortune into good fortune. How does the letter episode in *Hamlet* follow the old plot idea?

3. In previous scenes we have been told about the King's plot on Hamlet's life. Once again Shakespeare reminds us that the big scene is coming. Which minor character does he use to make the announcement?

4. Though the King has a foolproof scheme for killing Hamlet, the plan fails for two main reasons. What are they?

5. Notice that Hamlet was the one first wounded by the poisoned rapier. Why is it necessary, dramatically, for Laertes to die first?

6. Have we been prepared for the Queen's insistence on drinking the poisoned cup? How does her death at this point speed up the already feverish action? The order of deaths is Gertrude, Laertes, Claudius, and Hamlet. Is this order dramatically sound?

7. A clear indication of Hamlet's basic problem in killing the King is the court's reaction in line 331. They immediately and instinctively cry out, "Treason!" Hamlet has always been concerned lest his actions be misinterpreted. He is no murderer in the sense that Claudius is a murderer. Note that Laertes explains, for the court's benefit, "He is justly served." Whom does Hamlet urge to tell his story to the world?

8. Why does Shakespeare have Fortinbras come in just after the death of Hamlet? Why not earlier? Why not much later?

9. Note that Shakespeare, like a good dramatist, ties together all loose ends. What news does the ambassador bring in lines 384–387?

10. Many modern critics see *Hamlet* as a religious play, in which evil, sin, guilt, and atonement are crucial elements in a grand cosmic plan. To many critics, the mystery of *Hamlet* is the mystery of life itself. How do *you* see the play. Do you see it as a play of action, with the motives fairly clear and the delays explainable? Or do you see it as a kind of spiritual struggle between the forces of good and evil? Or do you see it, perhaps, as a combination of both? Explain your point of view.

CHARACTERIZATION

11. How does Horatio show himself to be a wise counselor in lines 76–77?

12. Notice that Hamlet is still finding justification for his intention to kill the King. (lines 68–75) What insight do these lines give us into Hamlet's character?

13. What kind of person is Osric? (Note Hamlet's opinion of him in lines 90–94.) Note how Shakespeare brings this character to life even though he appears for a brief time. When Hamlet uses double-talk in lines 116–123, Osric replies in all seriousness. What does that tell us of Osric? How does Osric himself talk?

14. A few touches are added to the characterization of Gertrude in lines 290 and 295. How?

15. Hamlet asks Laertes' pardon in lines 217–235. Why is this speech ironic in view of the coming events?

16. In his reply to Hamlet (lines 236–244), Laertes gives no indication of the plot he is engaged in. How does his character contrast with that of Hamlet?

17. The King remains a powerful antagonist to the very end. How does he introduce the poison in a perfectly innocent way?

18. Why does the King's confidence start oozing away as the fencing match progresses?

19. Does the Queen accept the reality of Claudius's evil at last?

20. Although the King sees his empire falling to pieces around him, he retains his drive for self-preservation until the end. How is this shown in lines 316 and 332?

21. Why does Laertes confess to the plot? Does he redeem himself by this act, or is the confession merely a dying man's desire to be pardoned?

22. How does Horatio show his love and his heroism as Hamlet lies dying?

23. How does Hamlet, in his death scene, show a consistent characterization with the Hamlet we have come to know in the play?

24. In *The Shakespearean Imagination*, Norman N. Holland considers Horatio the man of thought, Fortinbras the man of action, and Hamlet a man of thought and of action. Holland says, "At the end of the play, the man of thought and the man of action stand, facing each other, separated, divided; between them lies the man who was both, a failure precisely because he was both." Explain this quotation and then give your own reaction to it.

25. Some critics have considered Fortinbras a noble young man, particularly in his behavior at the end of the play. In *Motiveless Malignity*, Louis Auchincloss takes a contrary view. He says that after the death of Hamlet, "The kingdom of Denmark is turned over to the tender mercies of the brutal Fortinbras." Is there any support for the Auchincloss point of view? What is your attitude toward Fortinbras?

STAGING AND DIRECTING

26. In line 79 Richard Burton snapped his fingers when he said, "One." Is this a sound piece of business to add?

27. Some productions of Hamlet have the Queen applaud when Osric says, "A hit" in line 281. Is such an action consistent with her action to this point?

28. On the Shakespearean stage the apron had no curtain. Thus there could be no quick curtain to end a scene. When a Shakespearean character died on the apron, he had to be carried off! Note that Hamlet is carried off, as are the bodies of all the others. Some directors have drawn a modern-day curtain on the final scene. Others have included the "dead march." Olivier's movie version had a long, dramatic scene showing Hamlet's body being carried through the dismal castle halls. Which method would you consider effective?

29. Shakespeare often provides stage directions in the dialogue itself. What, for example, are Hamlet and Horatio doing in lines 352–354?

30. Directors are concerned with realistic problems like "How can we hold the audience's attention to the very end?" The usual method is for Hamlet to be half reclining throughout much of lines 341–371. Another method is for Hamlet to remain standing during his death scene and to fall to the floor only after saying, "The rest is silence." Which would you prefer?

31. Line 78 is worth spending some time on. In saying "the interim is mine," is Hamlet at last showing a cold-blooded resolution to kill the King soon? If so, how should the line be read?

32. Osric's role is a short one, but it is a colorful one. Read aloud two successive speeches of Osric and Hamlet (for example, lines 109–123) to show how Hamlet mocks this yes-man. (He has already called him a "water-fly"!)

33. How would you read Hamlet's apology to Laertes, lines 217–235? And Laertes' reply? (lines 236–244)

34. How should the King deliver his speech as he drops the poison into the cup? (lines 283–285)

35. The King's comments on the action are a superb revelation of this complex man. As he sees events going against him, his voice should somehow suggest his growing dismay. How, for example, would you read lines 289, 300, 308, 316?

36. Why doesn't the King knock the cup out of Gertrude's hands? How does he deliver line 294? How does the Queen deliver her line, 295?

37. How does the Queen express the fear and shock of her poisoning in lines 317–318?

38. Lines 342–360 show us the two friends, Hamlet and Horatio, in one of their last moments together. How should these lines be read?

LANGUAGE AND IMAGERY

39. Lines 10–11 are often quoted. Is Hamlet being a fatalist here? Consider also lines 210–215.

40. Shakespeare writes poetry of great beauty and invective of great power. What is Hamlet's appraisal of Osric in lines 90–94?

41. When Laertes says he is caught like a bird in his own net (line 313), he is using an image similar to that in lines 225–226, Act III, Scene 4. Note the same idea in lines 336–337 and 396–401. The idea of the cheater cheated is an oft-repeated motif in folktales. Why is this a particularly satisfying theme?

42. In his last address to Claudius, Hamlet continues to use bitter, descriptive language similar to that we have heard earlier. Why does Shakespeare reintroduce this language at this point?

43. At an earlier point Hamlet feared death and the unknown. Yet he tells Horatio, "Absent thee from felicity awhile." Why does he equate death with happiness now?

44. The Fortinbras role is a small one, but it does give the actor some characteristically fine poetry to deliver. In lines 378–381, for example, Fortinbras compares death to a huntsman. What other fine lines are given to Fortinbras?